Devon's BEAT

AN AMAZING STORY OF STRENGTH, SURVIVAL, AND SAVING LIVES

ANGELA PARROTT
AND **TYRAN PAYNE**

CEDAR HILLS
Publishing

ISBN: 979-8-9877408-1-1 (Paperback)
ISBN: 979-8-9877408-2-8 (Hardcover)

The content contained in this book are true stories based on the lives of real people. Any similarity to other people or stories is merely a coincidence.

Printed in the United States of America.
First printing edition 2025.

Cedar Hills Publishing
19462 Rolling Hills Rd
Warsaw, Missouri, 65355

www.cedarhillspublishing.com

Dedications

Angela

To my hero, my son Devon Parrott, who has endured more trauma in his short life than most do in a lifetime. You are the strongest person I know, and have overcome so much. Thank you for allowing me to share your story, and helping me spread awareness to get more kids screened to save more lives. Thank you Dawson for being a good brother, and checking on him throughout the years. You two have spent most of your lives arguing and driving me crazy, but your love and support for each other is unwavering. Thank you to my husband Jason for being my rock during the worst times, for literally holding me up. Thanks for always staying strong even when it is hard for you. Thank you to all of our friends and family who have supported us every step of the way. I love you all.

Tyran

Thank you first and foremost, to Angela for reaching out to me and allowing me the honor of helping to tell Devon's story. Thank you Devon for allowing this story to be told. Even as a student in 7th grade social studies class, you did not want the spotlight on you. Your willingness to allow your story to be told in order to help others is amazing. Thank you to the rest of the Parrott family for allowing me a glimpse into your lives. Thank you to my beautiful wife Amanda for your help and always supporting me. It is my sincere hope and prayer that this book allows Devon's Beat to grow far beyond our imagination. I hope it is used as a launching pad to help families all over the country avoid the heartache of losing a loved one. Believe me, I know the pain.

PROLOGUE

December 4, 2012

Mrs. Cook — Devon's 4th Grade Teacher

Devon was in a group that went to the library to read with Mrs. Lynde (the librarian). His group was coming back to the classroom. Mrs. Cox, a long term sub for Devon's other teacher Mrs. Goosen, and I were standing in the hallway to direct traffic. He was walking right behind another student. I remember watching Devon fall, and thinking, "That's odd. He must have tripped on the person in front of him." I went to him and put my hand on his shoulder to help him up and he didn't immediately move. That is when it hit me, he didn't just trip! I shook his shoulder and he sort of woke up. He sat up in a daze. I was in shock! Nothing had ever prepared me for a student collapsing right in front of me. I remember Mrs. Cox said, "Oh my gosh, he needs to go to the nurse!" I had Mrs. Cox watch the kids and I walked him to the nurse. I was questioning myself. Did he hit his head, what just happened?

Nurse Teresa — School Nurse

As I took Devon's vital signs, checked his blood sugar, and asked question after question, Mrs. Cook was right there. As a school nurse, especially in a rural, small town like Lincoln, you have to be prepared for anything and you have to remain calm. During my assessment and our conversation, I found out that Devon had experienced something similar while watching cartoons when he was "little," as he put it. This was definitely concerning to me and I wanted his physician to know every little piece of information I could find to help his assessment. Kids just don't "pass out" for no reason. When I called Devon's mom, Angela, I knew I had to present the information as calmly as possible. I did not want her becoming so upset that she would be unable to get Devon to his physician. I dialed the phone.

"Angela, don't freak out…"

1

Birth

JASON AND I MET AND STARTED DATING in high school. We were young, in love, and just wanted to get our life together started. The two of us decided college was not the best option for us. We were married in 1999.

We had discussed having a family, but knew we needed to be a little more established. Jason had been working in Arkansas for his parents' rock quarry, when they decided to sell the business. Jason started to look for another job. We ended up in Osage Beach, Missouri.

I was able to get a job working at a bank. After my insurance kicked in, we were going back and forth about starting our family. We finally decided to not necessarily try to have a child, but we would also not try to prevent having a child. One month later, I took my first at-home pregnancy test. I was having a hard time believing the positive test, so I took several more tests.

Being the type of person who does not like doctors, I am a terrible patient. I do not like needles, pain, or any kind of discomfort. I also have a horrible gag reflex when it comes to taking medicine. Basically, I am a huge baby. I did not want to go to a doctor to do a pregnancy test.

Finally, I went. The doctor was telling me about what to expect and gave me a book about pregnancy. I said, "Aren't you going to test me?" The doctor asked, "How many positive tests have you had honey?" I told her I had more than five. She went on to tell me that they are pretty accurate. She could see that I was very nervous and did a test anyway. Next, she started talking about sending me to have blood work done.

I did not know I was going to have blood work done! I was young and naive. I turned white as a ghost. I had never had my blood drawn. I called Jason and asked him what to do. He told me to go to the hospital, and let them take my blood.

I did go, and just my luck I had a brand new nurse. She was very sweet and could see I was nervous. Unfortunately, my veins were nervous too, and did not cooperate. They were hard to find. She said she did not want to stick me again, and she was going to go get someone else to help.

The nurse asked me to hold the needle sticking out of my arm. I turned white as a ghost again. The nurse decided she did not want to leave me alone. Down the hallway we both went with her holding the needle in my arm and me crying. The next nurse found the vein and the blood draw was over.

As it turned out, my new doctor was perfect for me. She was patient and kind. She also made sure I understood everything. Sometimes I have a hard time understanding and processing medical situations. She was very calm and compassionate with me. I am sure that she went home to her family after every appointment telling them the crazy things her patient did that day.

Over the next several months I began to show and grew quickly. My doctor told me that the baby was growing fast and we needed to talk through some scenarios which might include a C-section.

I had already made up my mind that I wanted a C-section. I did not think I was tough enough to have a natural birth. My doctor told me that we would wait and see how things were going when the time was closer. She really wanted me to experience natural childbirth. I was still on the side of scheduling a C-section.

In addition to our lives changing with the addition of a child, Jason was looking for a different job. He had heard about one in Sedalia, Missouri. He wanted to pursue it, and scheduled an interview. This was an exciting time in our marriage.

We were so elated to be starting our little family. Our friends and family were very supportive and happy for us. The anticipation was building for the big day. As the months wore on, the baby kept getting bigger. It was hard to believe we were almost nine months into this pregnancy. Everything seemed to be progressing well. He was just growing faster than anticipated.

I knew the baby was getting close to coming. I reminded Jason of the name I had picked out for my first boy when I was 14 years old. As a teenager, I loved the movie "Little Giants." I really liked Devon Sawa. I could just see my little blonde haired, blue eyed boy with the name Devon. When I met Jason at age 17, I made sure he knew the name I wanted, and I even made him go and buy the movie "Little Giants" to watch it. When the time came, my boy's name would be Devon.

The birth did not go exactly as planned. Because of his size, the doctor decided to induce labor a week and half early. Throughout the process, I never dilated much. They decided I needed a C-section. I was glad for that decision.

Devon Lee Parrott was born on Wednesday, August 28, 2002, in

Osage Beach, Missouri. We were very happy with his arrival. Jason and I were very proud to be first time parents. Devon had dark brown hair and big brown eyes. Even though he was not blonde haired and blue eyed, he was perfect. To say we were overjoyed is an understatement.

Our joyous occasion changed quickly. The doctor was not happy with the baby's condition. Devon's umbilical cord was wrapped around his shoulder and kept him from being born properly. This caused him to have some discoloration. He was a little too purple for the pediatrician. My medical team was afraid that he could have an infection causing the discoloration. The doctor decided he needed to be transferred to Children's Hospital in Columbia, Missouri, to be certain everything was good.

I was devastated! Since I had a C-section, I could not go with him. They took my baby! I was a first-time mom, and they were taking my baby to a different hospital in a different town. Jason had to leave me to go with Devon and I was alone.

Actually, not alone. My family was there, but I felt alone. They took my baby and my husband. The explanation they gave did not make sense to me. I was told that they thought he could have had an infection. Thought? He had an infection! They took my baby!

I cried my eyes out. The pain was getting more intense. I was thinking I did not want to take pain meds. If I did not need to take them, they would know I was doing well enough to go see Devon. My mom was begging me to take something. She and the nurses knew I needed pain management.

The next thing I knew, I was in shock and could not function properly. I was shaking and in so much pain. I couldn't even swallow a pill or drink water. After several tries, and quite a bit of convincing, I was able to get the pain medication down.

A hospital volunteer lady brought me a plant. I told her hysterically,

"They took my baby!" She was very confused and did not know what to do. She just sat the plant down and left.

After two days, I finally got better and was able to get out of there. Jason met me at the door of the hospital in Columbia with a wheelchair. I was finally going to be able to see Devon!

As Jason wheeled me in, he was talking about his interview in Sedalia. He was saying that he liked the job. He told me that he thought he wanted to take it—interesting timing for this conversation, to say the least. I made it to Devon and he was doing fine. He did not have an infection and he regained his proper coloring. We were able to be discharged on Saturday. For us as new parents in a traumatic situation, it seemed like a very long four days since Devon was born. We were all glad to be going home.

Now we needed to figure out what we were going to do about moving to a new job in Sedalia. I was going to need to let my job know we were leaving. Little did we know that Devon's complicated birth would only be the beginning.

2

Normal Life

ABOUT A YEAR AFTER LIVING in an apartment in Sedalia, we found a property we really liked. We decided to purchase the house 20 miles south of Sedalia, outside of a little town called Lincoln. Jason and I were both from small towns, and we liked the idea of our boy growing up in a small town.

Devon's life as an infant and toddler had its ups and downs. He seemed prone to catching whatever bug was going around. He had more ear infections than we could count. Dev also had strep, some crazy viruses, and even mono at one point. When he was 2, one of his eardrums burst. For first-time parents, there were some challenges. Because of all of the stress from his sicknesses, we were pretty sure Dev would be an only child.

Devon did eventually grow out of his sickly infant years. He was a very intelligent little boy—possibly, too much for his own good. He had a very good memory.

He loved puzzles and could put them together quickly. I know that I am biased, but I was starting to think this kid was a genius. He was, without a doubt, way smarter than me.

By the age of three, he had memorized "Twas The Night Before Christmas." Being smart could also get him into trouble. He was a bit ornery sometimes.

At one point, we thought he might be color blind. Learning colors just seemed difficult for him. Then, one day I had a bag of M&M's. I told him for each color he could say he could eat that color candy. He knew every one of them. That little knucklehead had just been pretending not to know all of the colors. He knew his colors, numbers, and money.

I had been working hard to teach Devon our phone number. He was just not getting it. I kept trying and kept trying. Finally one day he walked up to me and just said it like he had always known it.

I was so excited. I called my parents, then Jason's parents. I told some friends. I then called my friend Angie. She laughed and told me that Devon had known the number for a while.

I asked her why he would pretend not to know the phone number. She wanted to know who I had told about him finally knowing the number. I listed all of the people I had called. Dev had told Angie not to tell me that he knew the number. He said, "She is just going to go and tell everybody." Boy, did he have me pegged at a young age.

When Devin was little, he was an old soul. From a young age he really took to the older ladies. I remember he'd go to the bank with me and make friends with all the older ladies. They all loved him and he loved them.

I had made the decision that another child was not in the cards for me. Jason agreed; parenthood was hard. By about the age of three Devon started asking about a brother. He had met a couple of older kids and was certain he needed an "older" brother.

I had to explain to him that his brother would be a younger brother, but he insisted he wanted an older brother. I told him if I did have a baby it might be a girl. That was a big, fat, "No! I want a brother instead."

Several months went by and Devon was still asking for a brother. One night after a bath he had an eyelash on his face. I got it with the tip of my index finger and said, "Here, blow and make a wish." He did and quickly said, "I wished for a baby brother Mom." Even Jason was starting to question having an only child. They were teaming up against me. It eventually worked, and they convinced me we needed another child.

After a few months of not preventing pregnancy, I was officially pregnant. Before we even knew the gender, Devon and I were really wanting a boy. We started planning like we already knew.

Devon, helped me name his brother, kind of. I enjoyed watching Dawson's Creek. Dev "watched" it with me. Out of nowhere one day I decided that was it, Dawson would be his name. I knew it was perfect. If I had a boy I wanted to name him Dawson. Dev was on board; we just had to convince Jason. He didn't need to know where I had gotten the name. Jason agreed on it; although, he eventually figured out where it was from.

On January 25, 2008, Dawson Lee Parrott was born. There is no doubt our lives were forever changed. Devon was very proud to have a brother—for now.

3

For the Love of Sports

DEVON WAS A VERY ACTIVE KID. In the spring of 2007 we decided to get Devon more involved in sports to give him an outlet for his energy. He was 4 years old and was already loving everything sports related. He enjoyed playing anything and everything with his dad in the backyard.

The first thing available at his age was soccer in Warsaw, about 10 miles south of us. We got him signed up and we were all excited for his first game. Dev seemed to be a natural in the backyard. What could go wrong? When gametime came, he was very timid and looked like he had no clue what sport he was even playing. That is what could go wrong.

After a couple of games his dad and I were working with him in the backyard. We told Dev he really needed to get the ball and kick it in the goal. "You are being too timid," I said. "So you want me to take the ball away from the other kids?" He so innocently responded, "I was waiting for my turn or for someone to kick it to me."

Oh! OK, this made it all make sense. From the time Devon could walk, we had told him to share. He understood not to take things away from his friends, and to wait his turn. It was nice to hear that he had been listening and learning. We also knew we needed to change his sports mindset.

Jason and I had to explain that competitive sports were different. We let him know, if the other team had the ball he was supposed to take it from them. Jason told him he could help his team, and the object of the game was to kick it in the other team's goal to score. We told Dev he could also pass it to other people, but only the players on his team. The concept of competitive sports did not take long to sink in. Devon was scoring goals in no time.

In Lincoln, 4-year-olds were allowed to start playing T-ball. This proved to be a good summer activity for Devon. By the time the games started, Devon was able to apply the understanding of competitive sports to T-ball. He seemed to really enjoy it.

We enjoyed Devon being involved in soccer and T-ball. It was fun to watch him grow and develop. Throughout the fall and spring he enjoyed his soccer team. We were definitely becoming a sports family.

T-ball came around again that following summer in 2008. Dev was able to improve on his skills. His speed and athletic ability helped him be successful on the diamond. It was fun watching him enjoy competing. He was getting better even though he was only 5.

That same summer, Devon attended his first State Fair Community College (SFCC) basketball camp. He absolutely loved basketball and really loved the camp. There was no question at this point which sport he loved the most. Coach Thomas, the SFCC men's head basketball coach, told Devon he had great ball handling skills and wanted to see him back playing at SFCC in 12 years.

Jason was a very good tennis player in high school. As a matter of fact, he was one of the best players in Arkansas. It was only natural to get Devon started in tennis at an early age. Dev attended his first tennis camp as a 5-year-old. The camp was held in Sedalia. Dev was one of the better players in his age group. His dad's love of the sport helped give him early exposure to it.

By the time fall soccer started in 2008, he was a natural. Dev was fast and competitive, "stealing" the ball every chance he got. That season he scored 18 goals in 6 games. He really enjoyed being on the field with his teammates. He played again in the spring, but that was his last season. Because Lincoln did not have a junior high or high school soccer team, Dev would need to switch to football as he grew older.

The summer of '09 would bring a big change in summer ball. Devon was now old enough to play baseball. He would be learning how to hit the ball from an actual pitcher. He adapted well that first season. Dev also attended tennis camp that summer. He took his tennis time very seriously. He even won a couple of tournaments. The highlight of his summer came at the SFCC basketball camp. That was still his favorite sport.

In the fall, Devon played his first year of youth football. He was in first grade and was on the 1/2 grade team. His role wasn't that big because he was one of the younger boys on the team. Luckily, we knew his coach Luke Beaman very well. His wife LeAnn was one of my best friends and their son Jackson was a second grader and one of the better players on the team. That year was very successful and they ended up undefeated and won the championship. Devon's role expanded as the year went on. He got several chances to carry the ball and catch a few passes.

Later that year Luke, the coach of the 2nd grade boys basketball team, invited Devon to play up a grade with Jackson's team. Because Luke had coached him in football, he knew Dev was a decent athlete.

Devon was excited to be playing his favorite sport. He did not get much playing time, but he was really having fun learning and growing.

Tennis camp, SFCC basketball camp, and baseball took up the summer of 2010. Unfortunately, this would be his last year to do tennis. Due to health reasons, the coach was no longer able to hold the summer camps. We were sad, but we had plenty of activities to occupy our time.

With the fall came his second youth football season. Dev was the big kid now as a second grader on the 1/2 grade team. He played wide receiver, running back, and quarterback. He got better every game. He loved it. They did well that year, but didn't make it to the championship game.

Jason and I decided in the spring of 2011 that we would coach basketball. We knew it was Devon's favorite sport and we wanted to give the 2nd grade boys the opportunity to play. That first season did not go very well. The boys tried hard and they improved. Later that season Devon was invited to play in some tournaments with Luke's team of 3rd graders. Devon's love for the sport was growing.

The summer of 2011 was more of the same. We spent the summer with baseball and Devon attended the SFCC basketball camp. The fall brought another football season. Devon was on the 3/4 grade team this season. Luke was again going to be his coach. Dev was one of the fastest 3rd graders on the team, however he ended up being the center. The coaches struggled finding anyone able to even snap the ball. The ability to shotgun snap was out of the question for most of them. At one practice the coaches said, "OK boys we want to see everyone shotgun snap the ball. Let's see who can do it best." Dev, in true form, took it very seriously and won the position. Not necessarily what we expected. Like most things he had already done in his life, he killed it! The team had another fantastic season.

The 2012 basketball season went much better than the first. The boys had improved greatly and worked very hard during the season. Devon was a very good leader for the team. We were able to finish that season undefeated. The summer brought another SFCC basketball camp and baseball season. This was a unique baseball season because Dev struggled with some illness that summer. Devon was now one of the best pitchers on the team and was hitting the ball really well. In one particular game he had strep throat. He still insisted on playing. At the end of the game he came to the plate with a chance to win the game. He was able to get a base hit that scored the game winning RBI. It was a fun night, but he was pretty sick afterward.

In June of 2012, Dev and his friend Gabe Merhens went to the Mizzou football camp. It was not exactly what we thought it would be, but we were glad we took him. He got to show off his skills and got to meet some of the players, even the center. Who by the way was much larger than Devon.

That fall brought another football season. Devon was a fourth grader and he was set to be the quarterback. Jason was head coach and that wasn't easy on either one of them. There were moments in practice that were very intense. Jason decided to give the QB position to another player. Things with Dev just weren't going the way he wanted them to go. Devon continued to work hard and ended up showing everyone, including "coach" he belonged behind center.

Practices weren't great but when he got into game time situations he went full boar. He became Jason's number one runner at QB. Dev probably ran more yards than he should have that year. We fell short of the championship, but was not due to lack of heart and effort from Devon. When he put his mind to it, he accomplished it. It was a great football season for Devon. I will forever cherish those memories. Dev and his dad "coach" will always have that special bond.

Late in the fall Devon was able to play up on Luke's basketball team in a few pick-up games in Marshall, Missouri. He was falling more and more in love with the sport of basketball. He was working hard and getting better. We were looking forward to another basketball season with his classmates starting soon. We were excited to build on the great season they had as 3rd graders the previous year.

4

December 4, 2012

ON TUESDAY, DECEMBER 4, 2012, I was at work. I owned a business in town, and my in-laws had stopped by to check in when I received a call I will never forget. I looked down at the caller ID and it was the school. I was not sure why they would be calling. When I answered the phone, it was Nurse Teresa, the school nurse.

"Angela, don't freak out. He is OK, but we had an incident at the school. Devon blacked out or passed out. We don't know for sure which. He was just walking down the hall and he kind of looked like he was swaying. Then he just went down. He's OK but he busted his lip. I don't want to tell you what to do, but I'd take him to the doctor if he was mine."

I was already walking out the door shaking and crying. Jason's parents watched my shop while I took Dev to the doctor.

Our family doctor assumed he was dehydrated, but decided to do some blood work to be sure. As we were walking out of his office, he said, "We can order an EKG to be safe and rule things out if that's what you'd like."

I am "that" mom. I definitely wanted to do more testing. I really wasn't nervous about the situation, but deep down I knew he wasn't dehydrated.

Devon was very active. He pretty much ate and drank the same types of things every day. On this particular day, he was just walking down the hall and this happened. All of this did not make sense to me.

On Thursday, December 6, 2012, we took Devon to Children's Mercy Hospital in Kansas City, Missouri. Just to give you some context: we live in Lincoln. It is 102 miles to Children's Mercy Hospital from our house.

Jason's mom and dad decided it would be helpful for them to go with Dev and me, and Grandpa drove. Jason could not go with us to the appointment. In the end, it was much appreciated and actually much needed that Grandpa decided to drive.

I truly didn't know what to expect. I was oblivious, nervous, and anxious. Oblivious to the fact that something could actually be wrong with Devon's heart. Nervous to know where to go, what to do, and what to expect. Lastly, anxious for it to just be over. Devon, who felt completely normal now, expected nothing. Afterall, he was feeling great and appeared to be a healthy ten-year-old.

Check-in went relatively smoothly. In the exam room, the procedure went quickly. The medical team hooked him up to an electrocardiogram (EKG), to record the electrical signals in his heart. The technicians worked it like a routine patient. We were literally in and out in 15 minutes.

When they were all done with the tests, we headed to the car to leave the hospital. We knew that it would take a while for the doctors to read the test results. We were driving out of the parking lot and I was discussing with Jason's parents about how well the test went. We were exiting the parking garage, headed on our way home when I got "that" phone call.

"Hi, Mrs. Parrott, are you Devon's mom? Devon's EKG was abnormal. We need him to refrain from any physical activity until he is seen by our doctor."

I hung up the phone and was a bit shaky trying to explain this to Grandma and Grandpa. I called Jason. He too was worried and confused. None of us understood what could be abnormal. Everything seemed to be fine and had gone very smoothly.

Grandpa quickly knew we did not need to leave Kansas City. We needed to know more information. He took us to a local coffee shop. We waited there until we could get more details.

We got a call from Devon's pediatrician in Sedalia. He seemed equally confused. Children's Mercy called and said the appointment was set for the next week. All we knew at this point: Dev needed to be careful. He was to refrain from any athletic activity until the appointment.

This was a lot to take in. We eventually headed home, scared and leery. I can truly say I am so thankful for Grandma and Grandpa taking us to Children's Mercy for the EKG. I didn't know it was necessary, but it definitely was. I could not have driven home by myself with all of that information, and the questions swirling around in my head.

Abnormal? What does that mean? I was extremely concerned and freaking out. Many of my friends calmed me down. They thought it was just a heart murmur. Lots of people have irregular heart beats. It would be OK!

I was not OK. Just like any mom, I was worried. My brain would roll possible scenarios over and over in my head. What if it was serious? What if it is just a murmur? This played out over and over in my mind.

That weekend we were supposed to go to a family wedding in Iowa. Honestly, I didn't even want to go. The mom in me just wanted to have him sit still and do nothing all weekend. After all, they told me he couldn't be active. I was afraid something was going to happen to him.

We ended up attending the wedding anyway. In the end, I was glad we went. It got our minds off of the situation, and we had fun. More importantly, Devon had fun. It was good for all of us to enjoy ourselves and our family.

5

He Has What?!

ON TUESDAY, DECEMBER 11, 2012, we were not prepared for what we were about to hear. I had convinced myself that it wasn't a big deal. I just knew everyone was right. He probably had a small heart murmur, and it was going to be fine.

We walked into Children's Mercy with an open mind. As soon as Dr. T. walked in and started talking, we were blown away. Dr. T., was blunt and completely honest. She walked into the room and said:

"I am sorry, but your son has a life-threatening condition called Long QT syndrome (LQTS). Based on his symptoms and findings, he is at high risk for unexpected cardiac arrest. At this time, he can no longer be active in sports, and needs to be monitored 24 hours a day, seven days a week. He can be by himself when going to the bathroom and having a shower, and these with close monitoring from your part. We will apply to get you an automated external defibrillator (AED) to be at his side at all times. "

Wait WHAT?! He has WHAT?! We felt lost, and so scared. I was bawling! I looked over at Devon and he was crying. This very blunt, very harsh doctor said, "Oh no! Devon, why are you crying? You are alive. This is a blessing."

He simply said, "I can't play sports!" He sobbed. I sobbed. Jason was sobbing. We were very scared to lose our son. Devon was upset to lose his sports life. But most of all, we each felt the fear of the moment.

She was blunt, rude, and seemed uncaring. She didn't seem to understand how he felt. Dev was not happy about living this life, this life without sports! It was very clear that Dr. T. did not understand the time and commitment it takes to be a sports family. She also failed to consider the impact of how losing sports would be for a ten-year-old boy.

My heart was pounding out of my chest. I was trying hard to get it together and get some composure. Each time I would get it together, I would fall apart again. This just kept happening like a vicious cycle.

Jason was able to pull himself together better than I was. Thank goodness! He was able to try to comfort Dev after this heartbreaking bombshell had been dropped on us. We just sat in the conference room of the hospital trying not to completely fall apart.

The shock of this news, after thinking it was going to be a heart murmur, was devastating. I just kept thinking over and over, "What was she talking about? What was she saying?" My strongest instinct was to protect my child. However, I was trying to get past my own devastation. How could this doctor just matter-of-factly break such awful news to us. I was having such a hard time understanding and processing all of this.

I wanted this to be a dream. I wanted to just wake up and realize it was a nightmare. Unfortunately, that was not the case. We were awake and it was actually happening to my family, my son.

6

LQTS

ON THE WAY HOME from Kansas City. I tried super hard not to lose it. Try as I might, I was not successful. Jason was strong. He worked to get me to stop crying. He said, "Be strong for Dev." I tried and tried, but it was too much. In the end, I could not be as strong as Dev or Jason.

We had so many people to text and call. First was our parents. They were devastated, as well as confused. It was extremely hard to understand. It is hard to explain something that you do not fully understand yourself.

Next, we notified close family and friends. No one understood; no one knew what to do. Not only that, absolutely no one knew what Long QT syndrome was.

One of the first people to text me after the appointment was LeeAnn. Being one of my closest friends, she was devastated. Jackson, her son and one of Dev's best buddies was taken back as well. Her daughter Lexi and her husband Luke were also very concerned.

That night I spent most of it crying and researching LQTS. I spent hours looking on the Sudden Arrhythmic Death Syndrome(SADS) website. I was trying to figure out what was next. What were we going to do from here?

Dr. T. told us that in her findings, Devon had a very, very long QT interval between his heartbeats. He also had abnormal T waves. This is what led to his losing consciousness. He was at risk of more frequent occurrences if not treated.

According to The Cleveland Clinic, "Long QT syndrome is a problem with the electrical system in your heart taking too long to recharge. This issue can lead to a life-threatening type of abnormal heart rhythm. People can inherit or acquire Long QT syndrome. Most people take medication for LQTS. Others may need a device or surgery to lower their risk of abnormal heart rhythms."

The condition affects the repolarization of the heart after a heartbeat, giving rise to an abnormally lengthy QT interval. In layman's terms, the QT interval is the time in between your heartbeats, when the heart is recharging. LQTS patients have too long of a distance in between heartbeats. It results in an increased risk of an irregular heartbeat which can cause fainting, drowning, seizures, or sudden death.

I learned so much, too much. I was terrified! I was reading stories many people told me not to read. I had to do it. I had to find out as much information as I could. I did not want to miss a thing. I did not want to forget why we needed to keep a close eye on Devon.

7

Sadness and Mourning

THE DAYS AFTER THE INITIAL APPOINTMENT were filled with fear and many tears. I had to tell the story over and over again. I would explain to people what this condition was and what it meant. Slowly, I was beginning to understand it better so I could communicate what Long QT syndrome was.

Lincoln, a town of 1,100 people, was shaken. Our closest friends were fearful and unsure of what to do. Devon's teammates and friends were scared. Everyone was very upset for him and worried about his future.

I do not take for granted the effect this had on Dawson. He was worried about Devon. We had to tell him things no five-year-old should have to think about. Things like, "If your brother ever passes out, you have to get an adult ASAP." I had to teach him how to call 911 and what to tell them.

One of the days I was gone to take Devon to a doctor's appointment, a lady came by the store. She was a photographer. She had just heard about Devon's diagnosis. She had gone to a few of his football games and had some great action shots of Devon.

When she was taking the pictures we did not know it was his last time to play football. When I got back to work from the appointment, the photos were there. They were perfect, but awful. I hid them in the drawer, and I just cried and cried.

We were very scared! But at that point the sadness had taken over. Yes we had Devon, we were blessed. He was devastated, and we were all mourning the loss of sports.

If you are from a sports family you get it. There is a great sacrifice. There are many rewards and many lessons learned. For those who are not sports families, it is hard to understand.

Jason had already started coaching Devon's basketball team that season when we received the devastating news. As a result of the diagnosis, Devon could not play. Jason made the tough decision that he was going to find them another coach.

Devon, at 10 years old and wise beyond his years told Jason, "Dad please coach my friends one more year, they need you. I will be there to help you and support them."

How could this ten-year-old be more mature than me? I didn't want to go to the games. I didn't want to watch other kids do what Devon could not do anymore. But we did. It was really hard, but I am so glad we did.

The last home game of the season, we decided to put Devon in one last time. We all needed closure. It would be just for a few minutes, to make his very last basket. Basketball was his absolute favorite sport; he was going to miss it.

Devon needed this. We needed this. The town and his team needed this. Dawson, at five years old, was super excited. Daws was also very worried about Dev playing in the game.

Let me tell you, it took a minute. That kid could not make a basket at first. His team just kept feeding him the ball. It was kind of funny looking back, because he was in way longer than we intended. He even had to play defense a little. The other team rebounded his missed attempt.

I wish you could've seen how excited everyone was when Devon made that shot. I can still see through tears the way his team looked, the way his brother looked, and I can hear the crowd cheering!

It was a beautiful moment. When that ball went through the hoop, there was hardly a dry eye on the Lincoln side. Devon was very content and so thankful for that memory. Watching him made me thankful too.

8

A Second Opinion

THE NEXT SEVERAL MONTHS was a waiting game. Devon had several appointments. He had to do genetic testing. It took months for the results to come back. Jason and I had to be tested. Being a possibly genetic disease, it had to come from one of us or so we thought.

Dawson had to get an EKG and echocardiogram, but he was cleared. We were told he did not have Long QT syndrome. There was a 50 percent chance if Jason or I had it that Dawson would also have it.

We were relieved that Dawson did not have the syndrome. Deep down so was Devon, but it also made him a little upset. He didn't want his brother to have LQTS; however he couldn't understand why he had to have it. If I am being honest, neither did I. Why was this sweet, smart, athletic ten-year-old having to go through this?

The genetic test for Devon was to tell us what kind of LQTS he had. There are several types of Long QT syndrome. The most common types are Type 1, 2, and 3.

Type 1 patients are more at risk while being active. A Type 3 patient is more at risk while at rest. While doing the most simple things, like sleeping, sitting in class and walking down the hall they are most susceptible. Dr. T. was suspecting Type 1 and 3 based on how Devon's T waves looked.

We decided to get a second opinion because we still weren't too crazy about her. Dr T. facilitated the visit with her colleague, a second expert electrophysiologist in St. Louis. While the doctor had the same news, he seemed more sympathetic. He actually thought it sounded more like Type 3.

He understood the way Devon felt about losing sports, something Dr. T. did not seem to understand. She simply discussed his interests with him, and told him to take up the guitar or golf. (Eventually he became excited about golf.)

9

Our New Normal

I SPENT SEVERAL DAYS AFTER the initial diagnosis getting rid of things. Anything that was going to remind us he couldn't do the things he loved was no longer needed. We were having a yard sale. I was getting rid of sports equipment, including pogo sticks, jump ropes, basketball shoes, and cleats.

While I was packing all of this up, Dawson said, "Mom don't get rid of his cleats. I think he will need them again one day." Angrily I said, "Dawson we have told you this a few times, but your brother cannot play sports anymore. I am just trying to get rid of stuff that will make him sad if he sees it." Dawson replied, "Well I don't think he's done yet, so I think you need to keep them." The words and wisdom of a five-year-old.

While doing tons of research, I had a thought. How do we keep Devon involved in sports? We had all agreed that golf was a great alternative. Jason and Devon actually started going to play some. We even bought Dev some clubs of his own.

But, what else? One night it hit me. What about kicking? He could still be part of a football team if he could be a kicker. He would not be doing anything strenuous. It would not be physical either.

This became another way to keep me busy. I went to work researching kicking. Devon was kind of excited about the thought. He started watching videos and teaching himself the basics of the technique.

Oh my, kicking is hard! It is not something you go out and just do and you are good at it. I came across a guy in St. Louis, named David Brader. David had a business called Snap, Kick, Punt, and he offered lessons to train aspiring kickers and punters.

I emailed him about our situation and asked what he had to offer. We still had to wait for the genetic testing to come back and figure out the next steps, we were certain we wanted to pursue this kicking thing.

If he could just get good enough to earn the kicking spot, he could be back on the youth football team. I know that the coaches would have let him do it whether he was good or not. That is just who they are. But we were not made that way. If he wanted to do it, he was going to work hard and be good at it.

10

Raising Awareness

WHILE CONTINUING TO DO RESEARCH, I realized no one was really even aware of Long QT syndrome. My research also revealed it wasn't as rare as we thought. Awareness was just low. There were many stories about kids just suddenly dying, but no one was aware they had a heart condition until it was too late.

I was learning that conditions like LQTS were treatable. Some cases were even curable with the right procedures and medicines. Had some of these families known, their children might still be alive. They could have avoided horrible tragedy and loss.

Dr. T. had told us several times that Devon being alive was a blessing. His T waves were so abnormal and his QTc was so long that Dr T. told us it was a miracle he came out of arrhythmia spontaneously and did not need to be resuscitated. Everything in her vast medical knowledge told her he was lucky to be alive. She was surprised he did not have more frequent episodes.

We learned from Nurse Teresa at school Devon had experienced another unprovoked loss of consciousness due to arrhythmia, and at that time we thought that was a benign fainting. He was at home watching TV, a year before the big episode at school. He said he remembered feeling weird. The next thing he remembered was his dad waking him and asking if he felt OK. He had made some weird noise. He had no idea what happened. After it happened at school, Dev realized he had felt the same sensation.

With that, I decided to raise awareness. I held a small meeting of the minds in January 2013. This included a few close family, friends, and a few teachers who loved Dev. We decided to start a 5K run/walk/ bike ride.

Lexi, LeeAnn's daughter, came up with the name and design. DEVON'S BEAT! She sent me pictures of a heart with a heartbeat running through it. It was perfect!

LeeAnn was the main person to help me decide to have an awareness fundraiser. I am very glad I had her to lean on. Marsha, Angie, several other friends, and a few of Dev's teachers dove right in to get our first Devon's Beat going. One of Devon's 4th grade teachers, Anne Goosen, was very helpful.

I wanted to have the run/walk/bike ride sooner rather than later. I was told I probably couldn't pull it off by April 2013. But I am stubborn, and I was bound and determined. We set a date for April 6, 2013.

11

Life Adjustments

BETWEEN JANUARY AND APRIL there was lots of waiting, lots of appointments, and lots of tests. Dev had to wear several heart monitors. Doctors wanted to get a baseline to move forward.

Devon started a new medication and was doing well. I was extremely nervous to leave him alone. Jason and I moved his mattress into our room. There were many requirements, so many things no kid would want to do, but he never gave us any trouble. He did what was asked of him. I know he was extremely frustrated, but for the most part he never balked.

We received his AED and we were taking the device everywhere we would go. We had to have meetings at school to make sure everyone knew how to handle Devon should an emergency happen. Dr. T. even talked to and met with Devon's coach. We were thankful for everyone's willingness to learn all they could to help in an emergency situation.

Dev was put on a 504 education plan that outlined his care. I was asked to go on any field trips with him. Of course I didn't hesitate to accept. I did not want him out of my sight. His 504 plan stated all of the things he needed to do or not do. It made sure every teacher was aware of his condition, and that they knew what to do if he went into cardiac arrest. He needed more water than before and several snacks a day. All of this was listed in the plan.

Devon did several stress tests. His tests were leaning toward him being Type 3. Baseball season was approaching and it was the only sport he was content to give up. It was not his favorite.

One day, Devon got a big surprise from the basketball coach at SFCC. When Coach Thomas found out about Devon's diagnosis, he reached out to Devon's favorite basketball team, the Florida Gators. Coach Thomas knew a coach who worked for the Gators under coach Billy Donovan.

Coach Thomas honored Devon at a SFCC basketball game and gave him a signed basketball from Coach Billy Donovan. Coach Donovan had also sent Devon tickets to the Florida vs. Mizzou game in Columbia, and in the final surprise of the night, Coach Thomas presented Dev with those as well. It was a special night.

The night came for Devon to attend the Florida/Mizzou game, and things got even better from there. Luke and LeeAnn had a couple of front row tickets. Their son Jackson and Devon were allowed to sit in those seats for the game.

The two boys could be seen on ESPN photobombing a shot. During a break, Dev with his Gator gear on and Jack with his MU gear on were battling back and forth with who was number one. Devon then fell out of his seat, and it was all caught on camera by ESPN.

The next day I received a text that Dev and Jack had been on ESPN. Sure enough, they made three different segments. Devon falling out of his chair was #7 on Not Top Ten, #3 on Unite UFAIL, and # 1 on "12 things you may have missed last night." They said , "You have to look both ways to cross the street, but just ask this kid, you have to look all four ways to find your seat."

12

The Results Are In

IN MARCH, DEVON'S GENETIC TEST came back positive. He had Long QT syndrome Type 3. When exercising, his QT interval was shortening appropriately. It was before and after the exercise he was at risk for arrhythmias.

What did this mean? At first we were kind of relieved because it showed activity was not as dangerous for him, however it wasn't that simple. Since he was at risk more at rest, that meant the issue was all of the time he was not exercising. This included when he was asleep. Watching him during the day was not a problem. The issue was not knowing if he went into cardiac arrest when he was asleep. You hear of people going to sleep and never waking up. This was our new nightmare.

Dr. T. had a hard decision to make. She was really taking extra time to study Devon's case. He was only 10 years old. It was not easy to implant an ICD that he would eventually outgrow.

An ICD is an implantable cardioverter-defibrillator that will shock his heart and potentially save him if needed. It can be implanted transvenously or subcutaneously. For Devon, transvenous was the best bet. This type of device also had the highest risks. Because of his age, Dev would have more risks along the way when it had to be replaced.

Dr. T., who was actually growing on us, decided this was not a decision she could make on her own. We found out a couple months into the process that Dr. T. was a world renowned Long QT syndrome specialist. She attended and even led LQTS conferences all over the world.

She took Devon's file with her to one of her conferences and leaned on other LQTS specialists. After consulting with her other electrophysiologist colleagues, it was decided that a transvenous device was the best option for Devon. He was at too high of a risk for cardiac arrest during sleep. He needed an ICD implanted as soon as possible.

13

Lean On Me

DEV'S SURGERY TO IMPLANT THE ICD was scheduled for June 2013. These months of waiting were some of the worst times in our lives. We had to learn to deal with our new normal. Continuing with all of the requirements until the ICD could be placed was hard. We were constantly watching him for any sign of problems.

Devon's family, friends, and teachers were all sad for him and very worried. One of Devon's closest friends, Gabe, didn't even want to finish basketball because Devon couldn't play.

No one knew what to say. Gasbe's mom Marsha cried with me and was there when I needed her. My close friend Angie, like a second mom to Devon, was devastated too. Many people reached out and just couldn't believe what was going on.

Another sad moment for Devon was thinking he was going to miss field day at school and basketball camp at State Fair Community

College. We talked to his teachers and doctor, with me and his AED in the stands, he was able to do both.

At field day, he ran the races and even won some ribbons. This was a fun day. He was able to compete one last time in these events, and it was good for his competitive spirit.

When he went to basketball camp, he couldn't do very much. Coach Thomas made sure to find things for him to do. One of those things was being his partner in the shooting game knockout. They won of course, and it made Devon smile so big.

Before, we had taken for granted the ability to get to participate in these events. Now, it was a huge blessing to have the love and support from the community and our school family. We enjoyed seeing Dev get to participate.

14

5K

ON SATURDAY, APRIL 6, 2013, we hosted our first Devon's Beat 5K. Devon's basketball team came together and rode bikes with him since he couldn't run. Devon's older friends ran the race and lots of locals including teachers, family, and friends came out to run and walk. A few strangers showed up to participate. They simply wanted to come support the cause. It was beautiful. We got several wonderful donations and sponsorships. Coach Thomas and several SFCC basketball boys showed up to walk.

It was a big day for Lincoln, and we raised around $10,000. Ten thousand dollars? In Lincoln, Missouri? This small town really rallied around our family and our cause.

I decided not to run or walk because I wanted to be around to help if needed. One of Devon's teachers and a student or two helped with the time clock. I got to watch every single person cross the finish line. To say there were tears is an understatement.

I could not believe how emotional it was, to see these kids and adults come together to help raise awareness for LQTS, something that could have taken Devon's life, but didn't. It was absolutely beautiful. It was such a blessing.

It was the first time I could really say, "Everything happens for a reason." I still didn't understand why, and was still angry my kid had to go through all of this. A smart, loving kid who did everything he was supposed to. Why did he have to endure so much pain and heartache? We understood we were blessed he was alive, but it still didn't make sense. For the first noticeable time, I could say there was a reason and hopefully I would know soon.

The first year of Devon's Beat 5K, my biggest goal was to raise awareness. However, deep down I was hoping to find a way to screen kids. We were told that Long QT syndrome could only be detected by an EKG. Once detected, parents could do testing to find out the type of LQTS. But the warning signs are fainting and death. Most of the time the first "warning" sign *is* death. It is not lost on me that my child's warning sign was fainting. Thank God!

After this successful event I was able to donate $7,000 to SADS. I started doing more research on youth heart screenings. I had a long road ahead. I was determined to help other kids and their families.

15

Dr. T.

AS THE MONTHS HAD GONE BY with extensive communication, Dr. T. realized we, as a family, were taking Devon's diagnosis very seriously. I would go to every appointment with my notebook and my questions. I would write down just about everything she said.

She finally asked me one day, "Are you a school teacher?" Hahaha, no way! She assumed that because I was organized, took notes, did my research, and asked questions, I taught school. I explained to her I had to do these things to stay sane and in control.

I have never been able to comprehend things I can't wrap my mind around. I do lots of research. I ask lots of questions. Sometimes it probably seemed like I am not trusting because I do my own research. It's not that I lack trust. I need to know as much as possible in order to understand these complicated medical issues.

What Dr. T. didn't know was that some of my research included reading memorial stories about families who had lost their children to an unknown heart condition. It would upset my friends to know I would stay awake all night reading those stories and crying myself to sleep. They didn't know it was my way to deal with trauma. I needed to learn as much as possible, to empower myself in order to know the things I could and could not do having a kid with LQTS. I never wanted for us to think everything was OK and normal when it wasn't.

One story I read was about a kid with the same condition as Devon. They never left him alone. Years passed, and he was doing great. One day they needed to run an errand. The kid begged not to go. He just wanted to sleep in. "Please! don't make me go. It won't take long. I'll be OK." he begged. A five minute errand turned into a nightmare. They came home and he had gone into cardiac arrest. He was gone. Had they been home, would they have known? Probably not. Can you imagine the what-ifs they asked themselves every day? Not me! Even Though I was afraid of smothering Devon, I did not want to forget the importance of being aware. He needed to be "watched" at all times.

I realize it seems awful. Who wants to be "watched" at all times? Devon was such a trooper and hardly complained. Yes, he had his moments. He got angry. But overall, he just knew I needed to be with him and keep him safe.

16

ICD

DEVON'S ICD SURGERY WAS SET for Wednesday, June 19, 2013. Devon was going to have his own personal life saver implanted in his chest. It was going to have one wire connected to a vein that was connected to his heart. Since he was so young, and an active boy, Dr. T. was going to place it under his muscle for more protection.

We trusted Dr. T. by this point. We were very nervous about this procedure and him having a foreign device in his chest. We knew Dr. T. was making the best decision for Dev.

It was scary to give my son to the team to take him to the OR. A multitude of things ran through my mind. I was really feeling my anxiety of not liking doctors and hospitals. As you already know, I need to be in control of the situation. When they took him away, I had to place all of my trust in the medical team's knowledge and expertise.

Devon was very relaxed and strong. He put on his brave face. I watched him walk away from us, hand-in-hand with his nurse, making jokes with her. He was offered a medicine that would take the edge off, so he wouldn't even remember going back into the big, scary, sanitized operating room. He declined, "I'm not nervous, I don't need it." Dr. T. was absolutely amazed at the ten-year-old little boy that stood before her ready to get the show on the road.

We had a big turnout in the waiting room. People showed up to support us. At school that day in Lincoln, and some surrounding schools, students and staff wore blue and orange (Devon's Beat colors) in support. I got many pictures and kind words. It was inspiring and uplifting.

It was a very long four-hour procedure. I was a wreck, but held it together, for Dawson. He had cousins there to keep him busy. But not an hour would pass that he wouldn't say, "Is Devon about done Mom?"

They kept us posted every hour or two. The last call we got was from the head nurse. She informed us that the surgery went great and they were about to test the device.

Test the Device? Yeah, I found out the day before. While he was under, after they hooked it all up, they were going to put him into ventricular fibrillation. This would test the device and make sure it was going to shock him back to life.

I did not want to know this! This was the longest part of the four-hour surgery. I could have done without that info. I understood they had to test it to make sure it worked, but that seemed really scary to purposefully put someone in cardiac arrest.

We got to visit with Dr. T. after the surgery. She went on and on about our brave little guy. He was very calm and collected. She told us about the testing of the device.

On the first test, the device was not set correctly and didn't shock. This is why they test them! On the second one, just like in the hallway at Lincoln elementary back in December, Devon convulsed himself out of it. He got his heart beating all on his own. Dr. T. was absolutely amazed. She never understood how Devon didn't have to be resuscitated in December. Finally, she witnessed it with her very own eyes.

She laughed and teased him, "Now is not the time. I am trying to work and test the device, I don't need your help," she said.

Finally, an hour later she had it tuned up just right and most importantly, the device did its job. Devon did great. The surgery was all over and he was off to recovery.

We loved Dr. T. at this point. When Dev was in recovery, she went to go check on him herself. She told us she didn't see him at first. She was asking, "Devon, where is my Devon? Someone tell me where my Devon is." She finally looked over and he was lying there awake with a big smile on his face. He had seen her first. She told anyone that would listen, "There he is, that's why he's my favorite. Look at that smile on his face. He is so happy to be here and always has a smile for me." It was official, we absolutely loved Dr. T. now! It was extremely hard in the beginning of our relationship. Trust is what got us to that point. She was literally saving his life and would forever be in his corner.

17

Post OP

HE SETTLED INTO HIS ROOM, and we were able to be with him. The anesthesia was making him not feel well and he ended up getting sick, which they did not want.

The first nurse we encountered during his stay was not great. She accused us of letting him eat before surgery. She was mad that he threw up. To top it off, she knew nothing about his condition. She tried to give him Benadryl to help with nausea. He cannot have that. How did she not know?

LQTS patients cannot have the same kind of medicines as everyone else. Something as simple as Benadryl can cause a prolonged QTc. It is one of the most dangerous over-the-counter meds to give him. Another danger was the normal surgical anesthesia they use. They had to use something different. He couldn't take the anti-nausea medicine either. This is why he was throwing up. In addition to Benadryl, Zeepac, Omeprazole, epinephrine, and many other medicines can prolong QTc.

Everyone thought he had broken his arm because he had to wear a sling. The sling was because he was not supposed to raise his arm above his head for six to eight weeks. I even had to get a little testy with the X-ray technician for trying to make him raise it for X-rays.

Not all of the staff liked that I was so involved. I made sure they did things right. He is my son. As his mother, I want the best for him. I was willing to ensure the best care possible.

Most of the staff was amazing. Dr. T. was very comforting. She told me I was his advocate and had every right to make sure he was treated properly. This made me feel like I was doing the right thing.

Learning that many everyday medicines were very dangerous for him made me very upset. These were medicines Devon had been taking since he was a baby. When he got sick we gave him cold medicine or Benadryl. These are some of the worst medicines for a prolonged QTc. Cough syrups are dangerous too. Several antibiotics can be very dangerous. Even something as simple as "laughing gas" at the dentist could be harmful..

Devon would break out in hives as a child. He was allergic to something, but we didn't know what. We would give him dose after dose of Benadryl. It makes me scared to think of what could have happened but also very grateful nothing did.

My kids never drank caffeine. I was just that mom, but thank goodness. Caffeine is not good for those with LQTS, and especially energy drinks. Something very important I learned was that energy drinks were terrible in general. But they are extremely dangerous for SADS patients.

Devon was not amused that I made sure to tell all of his friends the dangers of drinking energy drinks. I would give them examples of kids that lost their lives. Apparently, that wasn't "cool!"

18

Now What?

THE SURGERY TO IMPLANT THE ICD was over and he was on the mend. In six to eight weeks he'd be released to be a little more active. We had big plans to start golfing. I had also reached back out to David Brader with Snap, Kick, Punt.

We talked about going to St. Louis when Devon was released. We wanted to try to get a lesson. I feel like all he had been doing was waiting and waiting for the last six months. Yet, here we were waiting again for him to recover.

It wasn't all bad though. He got to attend the Tim Barnes football camp in Lincoln and be his "helper." The Barnes family was kind to Devon. Tim had played center at Mizzou and was playing for the St. Louis Rams. Tim grew up in a small town north of Sedalia called Hughesville. I was able to connect with Tim's wife Lindsey at the camp. The two of them really made Dev feel special since he couldn't participate.

Devon also went to watch his little brother at the SFCC basketball camp. Coach Thomas made sure to have Dev help with different things, like setting up drills, monitoring the time, and making sure balls were available. This was a great way to keep him involved when he could not physically participate.

He got tired of wearing the sling because of his left shoulder restrictions, and me freaking out every time he moved his arm. We went to the doctor for our seven-week check up and we were a little disappointed. We had to wait another week per doctor's orders. Dr. T. wanted to make sure he had the complete 8 weeks to heal properly. One more week to not raise his arm, one more week to sleep in a sling, one more week of no jogging, no bike riding, and no swimming. Devon had also been very good about taking his prescribed medication so he could get released.

But then, on Wednesday, August 14, 2013 the eight weeks were up! That morning Devon woke up, stretched real big with both arms above his head, and had a huge smile on his face. He felt free.

We went to the football field first thing. He jogged to get his football after each kick. All with a big smile. He went to a friend's house and got to go swimming. I told him he could get in, but no jumping, diving, going under, or rough housing. Devon said, "So I can submerge my incision? It will be more fun than I have had in a pool in over eight weeks." Such a positive little guy!

That night Dev went to bed with no sling and a smile. The next morning he woke up like it was the only night he truly rested . He went to grandmas that day. She was going to take him to ride his bike. Dev and Grandma stopped by the shop during their bike riding adventure!

He was doing everything he was released to do all at one time! Dev was very excited to be "free" again. It was good to see the excitement on his face. I was happy to see that active boy back.

The doctor told us we had to start small. We needed to see how much he could do. Everything seemed to be going well. I am not sure we started small though.

We went back to Children's Mercy for Devon's follow-up appointment. The ICD was truly amazing. When we got in the room they hooked him up and read the device. It would tell Dr. T. if he had any episodes. Which he didn't. It showed his heart rate from June to July. She was able to tell that he was more active in July! Oops! Sorry, not sorry.

They raised his heart rate to make sure the device was still working, tweaked a few things, and said he looked good. His heart rate was going a little too high, so they did another stress test the next month. This helped to see if we needed to adjust his meds, again!

The bottom line was, Dr. T. allowed him to participate in a few more things, like P.E., but he had to wear a heart rate monitor and cease activity if his heart rate went over 180. She wanted it to stay between 160-180 during activity. He would be shocked by the ICD at 220!

Dev was ready to prove he could handle it. He hoped she would open more doors for him. He even had a padded under armor shirt that covered his heart and his ICD just in case she allowed him to play basketball.

Dr. T. told Devon that as long as he promised to stay safe and wear his padded shirt, she would allow him to try kicking lessons. If that went well, he could kick for the youth football team. This was a step in the right direction.

That was an amazing moment for us. He was able to get back to one sport he loved. No, it wasn't as a quarterback or center like before, but he was on a team again. Well hopefully, he had to get good enough first.

Dev was really a trooper. I hoped he would get everything he wanted from her. I was very hopeful that he could continue to be active. I prayed that Devon could prove to her that his body could handle it.

19

Finding a New Love

DEVON WAS READY FOR SCHOOL and his birthday! That year for his birthday invitation, I put "Devon is turning 11." But we were celebrating his first birthday—the first birthday of the new chapter in his life. We were putting the past behind us and celebrating the future on August 28, 2013!

We were hopeful he might be able to go back to doing sports activities from his past. If not, his future looked bright with a new lifestyle. We would help him adjust.

After he was medically released by Dr. T. to try kicking, we set up a weekend to go meet David Brader. It went well. He made sure to tell Devon all the things one could love and hate about kicking. He taught him so much, too much in one weekend. It was overwhelming for all of us, especially Dev.

When we showed up on Friday evening we didn't even have the right cleats. Turns out kickers and punters use soccer cleats. He went to David only knowing what he had learned on YouTube. He could toe kick the ball about 15-20 yards.

We took notes. Although it was a little harder than Devon expected, he did not lose hope. Before we left, David had a heart to heart with Devon. He told him that he needed to be mature and really think this through. He wanted him to decide whether he really wanted to do it or not. "Make sure you like it." Coach Brader said, "Your parents will put a lot of time and money into this, so you need to be sure."

We left Sunday with a new appreciation for kicking and big hopes that Dev was going to eventually do great. When we got home, Coach Luke said it was perfectly fine for him to kick. He wanted the kick to make it to the numbers at an angle to allow his kick off coverage to get there before the ball was returned. After a little practice with his new techniques, he was kicking it about 25 or 30 yards toward the numbers on the side of the field. The techniques were working, but it was hard.

School started and so did football. Everything was going great. He was the kicker for the youth 5th/6th grade football team. His first career kickoff was on September 9, 2013. He loved being back in the game, and so did his friends and teammates. Some of us moms were a bit nervous about Devon playing football.

He only did kickoff that year, until the end of the season. Luke let him try a couple of points after touchdown(PAT) kicks. He didn't make them, but was very close. All in all, it was a successful fall season.

20

More Freedom ... Kind of

ON TUESDAY, SEPTEMBER 17, 2013 Dev had another appointment and stress test. Jason was out of town and not able to go with us. This would be our first appointment with just Dev and me since his diagnosis. Once again he did amazing on his stress test! His medicine was working. They couldn't get his heart rate above 180, which was fantastic.

Dr. T. asked him about football. When she heard Dev talk about how kicking was going she was impressed. She released him to do almost anything. He could run, jump, play soccer in P.E., and do agility class.

When we asked her about basketball, she was not happy. Dr. T did not want him to play. She started out saying it was too much contact. We broke out the padded shirt. Her main concern was that his ICD could get damaged from contact and have another surgery as a result. Then she said that he wouldn't be able to keep a check on his heart rate. We showed her his wrist heart rate monitor.

Dr. T.'s final argument was basketball could be too emotional. Well, anyone who has had the good fortune to be around my son at some point in his life knows he is emotional about everything he does. He strives to be good at everything, sports, school, or otherwise. Devon is passionate, which in turn leads to emotion.

Dr. T. was surprised at me for trying to nurture the idea of basketball. She suggested why not another sport that was less dynamic with less chance of contact in heated, emotional situations. She thought that we just woke up and said, "Hey, maybe you can play basketball for the first time ever!" No, he had been playing since he was five. It was his favorite sport. We were trying so many new things with him, but Jason and I could not teach him to stop loving basketball.

I explained to her that we had done a lot of research that said kids with ICDs were still doing the sports they loved. I told her that we would be coaching. Jason and I would be in control of his playing time, positions, and more. She encouraged us to think about it more and pursue something else.

Wow, that was a bummer! We walked out of the appointment with our heads hanging. It was not fun. I could see the hurt in Devon's eyes. It took everything in my power not to sit down and cry like a little baby. We got into the car and he said, "It's OK Mom, you guys are doing so much for me. I don't have to play basketball."

I fought back every tear in my body and said:

"Don't you start lying to me now Devon. You have been honest with me about your feelings since the beginning. You have always told me what is on your mind, good or bad. I know you want to play, and we will talk it over with your dad. I will do more research, but whatever you do, don't start holding back on me now."

I got straight to work researching online. I started with my safe haven, the SADS website . I emailed my contact I had been using for information and support at SADS and confided in her. She gave me great advice and told me not to give up. She was also able to direct me to other helpful sites.

Jason and I discussed Devon playing basketball at length. If we were ever going to let him try, this was the time. We could be there up close and personal. The two of us talked about quality of life, and that it was Dev's life. We knew at that point that Jason and I could make decisions. At some point, Dev was going to get to weigh in on it. Maybe now we needed to let him have some input.

We sat Devon down in the living room and asked him a very difficult question for an eleven-year-old. "If you can only play a couple of years, is it worth it knowing you may have to quit all over again?" He said, "I know what it feels like to have to quit playing basketball. I can handle it, but if I don't try I will never know if I could have done it or not. I don't like that feeling." Once again, wise beyond his years

Jason and I talked it over, did more research, and sought advice from other ICD parents. The two of us decided that we were going to let Devon try under our strict rules. We made clear the understanding that it was on a two year trial basis. If we thought it was too much, or he had an episode of any sort, big or small, he had to quit.

We wanted to be up front and honest with Dr. T. I wrote her a letter explaining that we didn't want to disobey her, but we made the decision that now was the time to let him try playing basketball. It was a long letter. It stated what we were going to do in order to make sure it was a safe environment for him. I also explained, if he could run a race or play soccer, we felt he could play basketball. He was at risk mostly at rest. Why wouldn't we let him try to do something active that he loved? Devon understood it could be just for a little while and for proper closure.

Dr. T. called me the very next day after she received the letter. She told me she knew we were good parents and would keep him safe. Dr. T. stated that she had always wanted to say yes and let him try. She thought it was really important for us to think it through.

We needed to know as he got older, and it became more physical, she might ask that he stop. Dr. T. wanted him to know that he could possibly have had to give it up all over again. She was worried about Devon's feelings and the emotional toll that she witnessed LQTS had taken on him. She admitted that the first day she had to tell him he couldn't play sports was hard on her too.

The doctor we did not think we liked, and honestly did not believe she understood or liked us, was now becoming a very special person in our lives.

All the ups and downs, worry, and sadness, we finally had something positive for him that was of his choosing. Yes, we got him into golfing and kicking lessons, but he really wanted to play basketball. It was a relief to our entire family.

The journey continued as we turned our once inactive athlete back to active. He went from running, playing basketball, football, and tennis to only being able to jog. Now he was running, playing golf, kicking for the football team, and playing basketball again.

Remember Dawson telling me Devon wasn't done with his cleats just yet? That five-year-old boy was right. Maybe he was done with those sized cleats and those particular basketball shoes, but Dawson knew it wasn't over.

21

Reflections

AS I LOOK BACK ON THE FIRST TEN MONTHS after Devon's episode in the fourth grade hallway, I get overwhelmed with emotions. When looking in the rear view mirror, it all came flooding back. I was sad, scared, devastated, relieved, depressed, nervous, and proud.

It is sad to think back on all the pain. I was scared of all the "what ifs" and "what nows." Watching Devon go through so much was devastating. I felt relieved that he was alive and able to get back to a semi-normal life. Depression came into play remembering how low we had been at different times throughout the process. I was undoubtedly nervous about the future and what it held.

Deep down in my soul I was proud. Proud of my son and the way he handled everything from the beginning. Proud of our community and how they had given unwavering support. Proud of Devon's teachers and coaches, for all they had done for him. Most of all, I was proud of our family for sticking together and making it almost to the one-year anniversary.

Devon was asked in an interview on KY 3 news, what has he taken away from all of this? This is the answer from an amazingly wise eleven-year-old boy: "When life puts an obstacle in your way, you have to learn how to go around it." We could all learn a thing or two from that kid.

During the football season of 2013, I had reached out to the St. Louis Rams. We had been taking Devon to Rams games since he was a year old. Now that we knew Tim Barnes and his wife Lindsey, we wanted to cheer for them even more. The organization surprised Dev with pregame field passes. He was able to go on the field before the game and watch the players warm up. It was awesome.

I had also reached out to Greg "The Leg" Zuerlein's wife and shared Devon's story with her. I told her I was glad Devon had such a great guy to look up to as a kicker, and someone to aspire to be like. After the game, Lindsey told us to meet them when they come out and we could see Tim and get pictures.

We didn't know it, but there was another surprise for Devon. Greg and his wife, as well as the punter came out too. Devon got to meet the Rams professional kicker and the punter that day. It was a memory he would cherish. Dawson loved it too!

The following summer, Greg's wife even sent me pictures of Greg leaving for training camp in his Devon's Beat shirt we gave him. There are so many good people in the world. We have learned that through all the highs and lows.

22

A Moment of Thanks

WE MADE IT THROUGH 2013. The year flew by and we had a lot of ups and downs. We were getting better at dealing with Devon's condition. I was doing better at not freaking out all the time. As I reflect back, I can see how this horrible thing to happen turned out to have many positives.

Dev was even getting to try to play basketball again. Everything happens for a reason. Devon was put on this Earth for a purpose, and I expected great things from him. I thought he had and would continue to help others without even realizing it.

I wanted him to know that I love him more than he could ever imagine. I couldn't be more proud of him than I was at that moment. This whole difficult situation made me realize what an amazing kid he was.

Jason was amazing through it all as well. Although it was rough on him, he deserves thanks for being upbeat and positive. One of his biggest feats was keeping me strong. 2013 definitely forced us to lean on each other and Jason's strength held us up.

Last but definitely not least, Dawson was a champ. He watched over his big brother even though he is the little brother. He always checked on Dev when he took a shower. He also asked him if he had taken his medicine. I knew he had to grow up and hear a lot of scary things that year, but I was proud of him for being brave.

We were extremely grateful to everyone for everything! Although we still had some hurdles to overcome, Devon was on the good side of a bad genetic condition. We needed to continue to stay positive. We began to try to fly through the obstacles as best we could. If necessary, in the words of Devon, we would find a way to go around them. Our family could not have made it through that year without a lot of support from our extended family and friends.

23

Basketball Time

ON JANUARY 4TH 2014, MY BIRTHDAY, Devon played in his first fifth grade basketball game. He was back, even if only for a year. He was over the moon! He could hardly wait to get on the floor.

I was a nervous wreck. Marsha was a nervous wreck. Truth be told, I think some of his teammates were kind of nervous too. I could see how happy he was, and that made me smile. It Also helped me to calm down some.

He played great, hustled but not too much. Dev was getting back part of his life that was taken away. There was one moment where he was hustling for the ball and got himself in a jump ball situation. I froze! I was holding my breath. He came away from the scrum with the ball. He looked at me in the stands as if to say, "Oops I forgot! Sorry Mom!"

When I was kind of scolding him after the game, he said, "Mom, I had it under control. I had my padded shirt on and I was turning my left shoulder (where his ICD was) away from the contact." I knew right then and there, while I was still going to be nervous every game, this kid had it figured out.

Dev's goal was to play ball, and he was not going to jeopardize that by doing something stupid. He was going to play hard, but play smart. I was going to have to learn to trust him. It took some time, but eventually I did.

We had a great season and even invited a couple of older boys to join us to play in two sixth grade tournaments. We were able to win! It was a blast having Jackson play with Devon again.

On January 28, 2014, I received a phone call that I had been waiting on for a year. We found an avenue to get heart screenings for our local youth. I spoke with a lady from St. Luke's Hospital in Kansas City. I was very thankful that LeeAnn thought to reach out to them when we first started talking about screening kids.

St. Luke's agreed to come as far as Clinton, Missouri to screen 40 kids ages 13-18. Clinton was 26 miles from Lincoln. But they were willing to travel 75 miles to get there. It was not perfect. Most of Devon's friends were 11 and 12, but it was a start. We set the date for October 25, 2014.

Now it was time to get busy planning for the Second Annual Devon's Beat 5K. We also started spreading the word about the first heart screening. Devon's Beat was scheduled for April fifth.

I was getting a little discouraged because people weren't really signing up very fast for either event. Good donations for Devon's Beat were coming in, but not many runners were registering. In addition, other than my closest friends, parents weren't really signing their kids up to get screened.

I had to remind myself that they just didn't understand. Besides, we still had plenty of time. With more time and awareness I knew we could get kids signed up to be screened.

I recruited some help spreading the word and promoting Devon's Beat. Once again one of Devon's fourth grade teachers, Mrs. Goosen helped organize another orange and blue day at school. If the teachers wanted to wear jeans, they could pay a dollar and the funds went to Devon's Beat. I knew I had the right people in my corner. It was just going to take time.

This was personal for Anne Goosen. Even though she wasn't there due to maternity leave, it had been her sub who watched Devon collapse in the hallway. Dev was one of her students, which made him like one of her own kids.

Devon also decided to try archery for the first time as a fifth grader. This was once again one of those things to keep him involved. Archery was something Dev could continue to do, if he liked it. It was fun to watch him learn how to master it. In the beginning, he wasn't great at it. In fact, the first time I watched him I was not impressed.

Another thing you need to know about me is I do not pretend my kids are perfect at everything. I am their biggest supporter and tell them when they do good. But, I also tell them when they suck. Honestly, when Dev first started he sucked!

It became boring for me, but I dropped the negative attitude and got to watch him slowly wrap his brain around it. Eventually he got the technique down and ended up qualifying for state that year. Once again I watched Devon not give up and give it 100 percent until the very end.

24

Accentuate the Positive

DEVON HAD ANOTHER DOCTOR'S APPOINTMENT right after his fifth grade basketball season finished. Again, he aced the stress test. Dr. T. was very proud of his heart rate when he was active. She read his device, and was very pleased he had no recorded incidents. When we told her he had just finished basketball season, she smiled.

She told him he did great, and granted him permission to play another year. What a great feeling! He had not only gotten to play again, but had proven that his heart could handle the stress. His reward for his hard work was another season. She warned him that as he got older it might not be that cut and dried. She told him to enjoy it while he could.

Did I mention we loved her now? At this point in Devon's eleven-year-old life he was learning how to love new things, and accepting that some things may not last forever. He was going to enjoy them in the present.

He was kicking for the football team, playing basketball, plus taking up golf and archery. He was slowly getting to what would be considered a "normal life."

The day-to-day worries and remembering to take his meds was getting old. But, he knew this was part of managing his condition. As time passed, he realized he wasn't cursed or being punished. He was simply glad to be alive. As the months went by, Devon was starting to realize there were plenty of other kids who weren't so lucky.

His life goals had changed a little. He had now decided he wanted to try to get good enough to kick in college. This would be a great way to cover some of the cost. He also thought he'd like to be a basketball coach. He was looking for any way to stay involved in the sport he loved.

Devon's Beat came and I was silly to worry. We had a great crowd. People showed up to participate and be a part of the event. We raised more than $10,000 again!

One of the donations came as a big surprise. I got a letter in the mail one day with no return address. I could see it was sent from Batesville, Arkansas. Who did I know in Batesville? It was about 45 miles from my hometown, but I was unsure. When I opened it in the driveway, I gasped. It was a check for $1,000. This check came from a friend I graduated with, Jarrod Krepps. I was brought to tears with his generosity. Other than seeing him briefly at our high school reunion in 2008, I hadn't seen him since graduation. The generosity I was witnessing every day was amazing and it couldn't help but make me a better person.

Devon ran for the first time at that year's Devon's Beat 5K. His time was 29.15 and he medaled in his age group. In case you are wondering, I was a nervous wreck. Yes! I cried when he crossed the finish line. I cried again when I gave him his medal. It was a beautiful day. Even Dawson ditched his dad and took off running to finish the 5K. Yes! Tears again!

By July I still had lots of spots open for the heart screening. I was learning two things. One, most of the kids affected by Devon's story were not 13 yet. Two, while I was doing my best, I needed to figure out a way to reach more people. I needed to get the story out to more than just "our group of people."

In July, I came across a KY3 NBC Springfield, Missouri, interview and it was about heart screenings. The interview highlighted a lady named Tammy and she was from Springfield. She was aware of a few kids who lost their lives from unknown heart conditions. Tammy had an imaging business that was a non profit organization. She gave free ultrasounds to expecting mothers who might not be able to afford them, and didn't have insurance.

She was offering screenings to young people ages 8-25! I thought, "This may be an answer to my prayers." While I was thankful for St. Luke's Hospital and was looking forward to finally offering screenings, I needed to learn more about Tammy and her heart screenings.

The other thing I was learning was very discouraging. Parents were admitting to me that when they approached their kids about the heart screening, they were too scared to do it. They didn't want to know. They didn't want to go through what Devon went through. What? That didn't make sense to me. He was alive because we knew. By now, even Devon was convinced how lucky he was.

I had a few parents confess to me they didn't want to know. They said, "If nothing seems wrong, why would you want to bring on more stress?" They were fine as they were. WOW! I was extremely upset hearing this. It made me realize they just didn't get it. We had to do something to make them understand the importance of getting their kids screened.

In their eyes, they saw and heard all the trauma we went through and wanted no part of it. Devon got his warning sign and was able to move on and live. These "perfectly healthy" teens in Lincoln hadn't fainted, they've had no troubles, no warning signs.

I decided to reach out to KY3 myself and see if they would be interested in doing a piece on Devon. On August 13, 2014, KY3 NBC came to Lincoln and interviewed Devon and me.

It was a very hard thing to do. I didn't make it through the interview without crying. They had me tell the events that led us to where we were. I told them how lucky and blessed we were to have Devon alive. The statistics at that time were one in 100 people had an unknown heart condition.

I explained that when we hear of these kids suddenly dying on the field, court, or in their sleep that it was largely from unknown, treatable heart conditions. I was doing my best to get people to see the severity of the problem. I needed to make them understand.

Devon did great in his interview. This almost-twelve-year-old bravely stood in front of the camera reliving that awful day and the bad days following. He told the viewers of KY3 how important it was to get your kids' hearts checked. That got things rolling better for the first heart screening. Before I knew it, we had 40 kids signed up.

25

Stacking Days

THE SUMMER WENT PRETTY WELL. We spent lots of time at the football field. Devon was determined to put in the work to get good at kicking. He knew it would open some doors for him if he became good at it. He also knew that he could not participate in football unless he was the kicker. Dev would kick and punt and Daws would run and shag balls.

We went to another kicking lesson weekend in St. Louis. David thought Devon was getting better. He gave him some more pointers and things to work on. Coach Brader was very helpful.

One day while we were at the field, there was an older kid out there kicking. I did not recognize him, but he was good. It didn't take long for me to spot his grandma, Mrs. Linda Cate, our elementary guidance counselor. It was her grandson Bailey Cate. He was from Florida and was visiting his grandparents. Bailey was a high school senior and was well on his way to a college football scholarship. He worked with Devon, and reaffirmed he was moving in the right direction.

I finally worked up the courage to reach out to Tammy, the owner of Midwest Heart Check. The phone call went great. I explained to her our mission and that while I was thankful for our upcoming heart screening with St. Lukes, I was really looking for heart screenings that would travel to Lincoln. I wanted them to screen kids as young as Devon's age.

The St. Lukes company basically only screened teen athletes. They saw them as the ones most in danger. In some ways, they are. However, Devon was an athlete, but he was most at risk when resting. That never sat well with me.

The only downfall with Midwest Heart Check was cost. It was more expensive, since it was a private screening company. We had limited funds. We only had two fundraisers and part of that money went to SADS.

We decided to offer a screening and pay for half of each child's test. This would mean the parents would only owe $50. It was better than not having screenings at all for that age.

Saturday, October 25, finally came and we met St. Lukes in Clinton. We were able to screen 40 kids. We had a couple of kids who needed to be looked at closer. One of these kids was Jackson, my friend LeeAnn's son, and it really scared him. However, all 40 kids were deemed healthy and cleared to continue playing sports.

It was a great day! Many of the parents were not only thankful, but they went home with peace of mind. We announced that we were going to have another screening in Lincoln with Midwest Heart Check on November 8, 2014. This was not a lot of time for everyone to sign up.

We ended up screening 38 Lincoln kids ages 9-29! It was a very special day. Many of Devon's friends and teammates were able to be screened. They did find four with abnormalities, but all were cleared to play sports. It was recommended that they be screened again in a year or two.

The weeks went by quickly, and before we knew it we were visiting family for Thanksgiving. During Thanksgiving, Bailey Cate came back to Missouri to visit his grandma and grandpa. He invited Devon to kick with him again. It was cold and snowing, but they did it anyway. Devon described it as the coldest he had ever been.

We had so much to be thankful for in 2014. The obvious thing that Devon was with us. Life was moving in the right direction. He was able to enjoy basketball. Kicking the football was really becoming a passion for him. It allowed him to continue to be involved with the team. He had learned two new sports with golf and archery. He was really settling into this new life.

26

Dance and Auction

OBVIOUSLY, WE EXPECTED BIG THINGS in 2015. We hoped for more things to be thankful for. After the previous three years, we felt like we were beginning to find a place and cause in our storm. For the most part, 2015 started out pretty well.

Devon was ready for sixth grade basketball and we had begun planning our Third Annual Devon's Beat 5K, with a twist. We knew that we needed to try to raise more funds to help cover the expensive cost of the screenings. I still wanted to be able to screen kids as young as possible.

My committee and I decided we were going to have a dance and auction in conjunction with the Devon's Beat 5K. We were busy trying to raise more money. This was going to help us get the screening company to come to us and screen kids. Word of mouth was spreading and screening was getting more popular. My goal was to be able to pay for all of the heart screenings. I wanted no family to have a burden on them with costs.

We traveled to Springfield and did a commercial and interview with Tammy from Midwest Heart Check to raise more awareness. Once again, Devon was great. He took it all in stride. He wanted to get the message out to as many people as possible, just like I did.

Our family also traveled to St Louis again for kicking lessons. On this trip, Dev had the treat to punt with a college punter who was hoping to go pro. This inspired Devon to work even harder. He was improving every time David would see him.

While we were busy planning our new Devon's Beat big event, we got word that Tammy was coming to Lincoln to join us. She decided she was going to offer heart screenings during and after the 5K. This was such a blessing for our participants.

In addition, we were going to have a special guest. Miss Missouri, Erica Stone, was coming to Devon's Beat to run and help raise awareness. Devon and I had met her at Lincoln Elementary School when she came to read to classrooms. She was very sweet and quick to want to help with our fundraiser.

On Friday evening April 3, 2015 we held our first dance and auction. It went great! Saturday we had our third Devon's Beat 5K. Both were very successful. It was fun to see everything come together.

Miss Missouri did not disappoint, and I even got to wear her crown while she ran. Devon finished in the top 10 with a 27.08 and lazy little Daws finished 20th overall with a 30.38! All with a smile on his face. It was a great day!.

We were able to raise $12,000 at the Devon's Beat dance, auction, and 5K. Twelve thousand dollars. Wow! I was overwhelmed. We quickly scheduled two more Lincoln screenings. One was set to take place in May. We were able to schedule the other one in June.

Devon finished his sixth grade year and was officially moving on to be a junior high kid. It was hard to believe that we had made it to this point. We were thankful for this time in his life and the life of our family.

27

The Summer of '15

THE TIME CAME TO DO the summer screenings. In June, we screened 31 kids. This was great; however, we needed to reach out and get to other schools. We planned to do so. In July we scheduled a heart screening in Climax Springs which is 35 miles southeast of Lincoln. We were able to screen 20 kids there.

Devon started his summer off as busy as ever. Because he was old enough now, he went to summer weights. We also attended more kicking lessons. He was 13 years old and kicking 30-yard field goals. Devon was able to sign up and play summer basketball as well.

Everything was going great until Saturday, the 25th of July. Devon was feeling sick and thought it was a stomach bug. He had woken up in the middle of the night throwing up and in immense pain. He was crying and yelling. He finally fell asleep. When he woke up Saturday morning he felt a little better.

It was time for youth football camp and Dawson was excited to start his season. I was hopeful Dev was on the mend. He was a trooper.

While I was unloading the car at the football field, I looked back and Devon was making his way up the ramp. He was walking slowly and obviously not feeling well. He looked like a 90 year-old man walking. As he got closer to me he looked green.

One of our friends said, "What's wrong with Devon?" By that point I was extremely concerned. I didn't know, but we were going to find out. I ran out onto the field and told Jason, "Dev isn't right, I think I need to take him somewhere." Jason took one look at Devon sitting in the stands and told the other coaches he was leaving to take us to the emergency room.

With Devon's heart condition, he is at high risk for a cardiac episode when he is really sick. Dawson stayed back with friends and off we went to the ER in Sedalia. Jason got us there quickly.

They did an X-ray and saw some cloudiness in his abdomen. They thought it was constipation. The ER doctor told us to give him a laxative. Since he was obviously dehydrated, they said to try to get him to eat and drink.

We tried, but he wasn't getting better. We packed him up and drove him to the Children's Mercy ER. He was slowly getting worse, and had a high fever. After an ultrasound and CT scan we were told he had a ruptured appendix. He needed emergency surgery.

With Dev medical care wasn't that easy. They had to contact his heart doctor and decide what he could and could not take. They also discussed what kind of anesthesia he could have for the procedure. We were told they'd have to turn off his device so he wasn't shocked during surgery.

What? What if he needs the device? We were very scared. Not knowing which medicines he could or could not have delayed his surgery. It was delayed further finding out about turning off his device or not. To add to the complications, he was forced to eat and drink, so he had food and liquid in his stomach. The doctors decided there was no choice but to wait until the morning for surgery. This in turn would put him at risk for a bad infection.

The next morning, July 26, the surgery happened. Dev came through all of that fine. Perfect actually. Again, he was very brave. His only negative moments were because he was thirsty and hungry.

The nights were kind of painful. The pain level caused his heart rate to go too low. The pain meds made this worse. It worried me. If his heart rate dropped to 50, he would need to be paced by his device.

I expressed my concerns to the staff at the hospital. They lowered his meds and added some regular Tylenol for pain. The nurses were wonderful. One told me to never stop being his advocate.

Both sets of our parents and several friends were helping with Dawson. Jason was coming back and forth from work after the surgery was done. Dev received lots of goodies delivered from friends and family. His nurses referred to him as a superstar.

They originally told us he would be hospitalized for five to seven days. After four days, he was doing well enough that he was discharged. We were happy to be home. Per doctor's orders, Dev had to rest. It was also important for him to blow into his breathing device to keep his lungs healthy and prevent pneumonia.

They had us watch for fevers or unusual pain. The first few days, although painful, went well. Slowly he was getting low grade fever, but nothing too bad. When we went to bed on August 4, he was feeling pretty good.

28

Divine Intervention

BACK IN 2013, I LOST MY COUSIN Crystal to cancer. She had four young children and she herself was too young to leave us. It was a very hard situation. I have struggled with it for years.

We were very close. When she first got diagnosed we were texting. I will never forget. I was apologizing for what she was going through and wishing I could do something. Crystal told me that she was fine, and that she was sorry for me.

Crystal told me she could handle anything that happened to her, but she could never be strong enough to handle her kid going through what Devon was going through. She had the nerve to call me brave! She was brave, but that was just who Crystal was.

She loved her kids and couldn't imagine them in pain. She fought a good fight. Crystal received a bone marrow transplant and was less than a hundred days from being released to go home to her babies. Unfortunately, she got sick and her organs shut down.

Fast forward to the night of August 4, 2015. I had a dream about my cousin Crystal. That actually wasn't uncommon, but this one was definitely different. In this dream Crystal was the cousin that was alive and we were mourning my other cousin's death. It seemed very real. We cried together. All of a sudden she hugged me in my dream. In my dream? It was so real it woke me up and I actually felt It. I had tears in my eyes.

I just sat there in the dark room and wondered if it was real or a dream. Suddenly, I panicked. Devon! I ran into his room to check on him. He had a very high fever! I woke him, he didn't feel right. I gave him meds and waited until the morning when I could call his doctor.

His fever went down, but the doctor knew something was not right. His pediatrician recommended we go to Children's Mercy ER as soon as possible. We got everything together and headed back to Kansas City.

In the ER we learned he had a very bad case of pneumonia. His lungs were full of fluid. There were also two abscesses where his appendix was removed. He was very sick. The ER doctor decided he needed to be admitted again.

The medical team ended up wanting to put him on two very strong antibiotics. The doctors were concerned they might have to drain his lungs and remove the abscesses surgically. The doctors had to get permission from Dr. T. to give him antibiotics. The two they wanted to prescribe were on the list of meds not to be administered to a LQTS patient.

The risks of major complications from pneumonia and abscesses outweighed the risks from the antibiotics. He was being monitored very closely by the staff. Dev also had his ICD in case of emergency. The decision was made to move forward with the high powered antibiotics.

He had a rough time with fevers every day while he was in the hospital. He had to change meds because they were prolonging his QTc too much. This put him at higher risk for cardiac arrest.

For a while, the medical team had been talking about changing daily meds to shorten his QTc. This was a very scary time. He really needed to show some positive signs of the medicines working. Eventually the antibiotics kicked in and started to do their job.

Finally on August 8, we headed home and he was on the mend again. On the way home, I kept thinking about my dream. I was thanking Crystal for waking me up that night, so I could give him Tylenol to help with his fever. I wasn't sure I even knew what happened. I could not shake the feeling she helped my kid.

We were absolutely exhausted, but Devon was getting better. He was a little upset though. He had worked hard early in the summer to get stronger and better at kicking. Now he was weak and had lost more than 10 pounds in about 15 days. As he got better, he realized he could get back to work and do just fine.

29

Movie Celebration

DEVON HAD ANOTHER APPOINTMENT with the infectious disease department at Children's Mercy. Although the pneumonia was still there, it was much better. The abscesses were gone. This was a relief to all of us.

The four of us decided to celebrate that weekend. On August 15, 2015 we set out for a day of fun. We took off for the movies. Dawson and I wanted to watch "Minions" and Dev and Jason wanted to watch "Mission Impossible."

Dawson and I were settled in with our popcorn. A few minutes into the movie, I saw a man at the bottom of the theater waving his hands in the dark. What the heck? It was Jason. He was waving at us, trying to get our attention.

Dawson and I quickly ran down there and he was shaky, but calm. Jason said that Devon had passed out. I was frantic. He told me he was

OK now. He said, "I think I saw his machine shock him." Dev was right outside the door crying. I was freaking out!

Jason got us all calmed down. We rushed out of the Sedalia movie theater and called Dr. T. as soon as we could. Unfortunately, she was out of the country. She told us to head to Children's Mercy ER as quickly as possible. Dr. T. told us to pull over and call for an ambulance if we needed to.

I was trying not to be hysterical. I asked tons of questions. Jason said they were eating popcorn, watching the movie. Suddenly, Devon's head fell forward, like he fell asleep. "Seriously?" Jason thought, "Asleep already?" So, he said, "Dev, you OK? Dev!" he shook him. Nothing. Then he saw Dev jolt a little and open his eyes. Then, he was out again… "Dev!, Dev!" Then he saw his body thrust. The shock woke Devon up and they were both scared!

We asked Devon what he remembered. It was little to nothing. He only remembered waking up, Jason carrying him out of the movie, and telling him he thinks he was shocked. Devon said he felt normal except for his tongue. It felt weird like when you put a nine volt battery on it to test it.

He started crying on the way to the hospital. We asked why he was crying. He said he finally got his sports back and she was going to make him quit again. I was scared and angry. Could he really be going through all of this again? Jason was scared, but calm.

Once we got to the hospital, Dr T.'s colleague checked him out and checked his device. It showed everything that had happened. He went into cardiac arrest because his QTc intervals were too long. The device gave his heart a chance to work itself out of it. When it didn't, it first gave him a mild shock. Then it waited, and finally determined it had to save him. Then he was shocked at full force. This was the jolt Jason had seen. That shock brought him back into normal sinus rhythm.

Dr. T. and her colleague decided they needed to try a new medicine to shorten Devon's QT intervals. They decided the new medicine was a necessity for Devon to live. The doctors wanted to start it ASAP. We were scared. He had to be hospitalized in ICU for a 48 hour observation.

This medicine had many possible side effects. The scariest one was that it could do the opposite and actually make him worse. Once again both sets of grandparents came and helped with Dawson and visited Devon.

The first round of medicine was brutal. It was liquid, and like me Devon had a really high gag reflex. He had always hated any liquid medicine. Getting it down was rough. Finally, he got it choked down. Meanwhile, they found a capsule called Mexiletine that was the same strength he needed, 150 mg three times a day. Now he was taking it three times a day and Nadolol two times a day and he was not even 13 yet. Hopefully these new medicines would shorten his QTc.

Thankfully, Devon had no bad side effects. After the 48-hours were up, he was sent home again. For the third time. He was still weak. However, Dev was "done" with Children's Mercy. We were counting our blessings, and extremely thankful that we knew about his condition. We were very appreciative that Dr. T. made the decision to implant that ICD. It literally saved his life.

30

Junior High

DEVON STARTED HIS FIRST DAY of junior high school on August 19, 2015. He only went to school for a half-day to start. He had lost more than ten pounds in four weeks and a lot of his strength. But, Dev was eager to get it back. It was scary for his teachers, friends, and coaches because he was frail and pale. Slowly, he began to put his weight back on and was starting to do some punting and kicking drills.

By September 1, he was fully released to go back to his normal activities. He was advised to go at his own pace and listen to his body. The medicine was working and his QTc intervals were shorter than they had ever been. He had even gained four pounds back.

Not wanting to waste any time, we made plans to attend kicking lessons the next weekend to get him back to where he was before the appendectomy and pneumonia. On September 8, 2015, Devon kicked off in his first junior high football game as a seventh grader. He worked hard to make it back for the first game. He was doing better every day.

We went straight to work sharing his story everywhere we could. On September 23, KY3 came to Lincoln again to do a story about the new events that happened in Devon's life. It was titled, "After cardiac arrest, Ozark teen beating the odds." Devon did such a great job reliving the worst couple of months of our lives. It was tough, but he knew how important it was to share this story. Dev knew that if he hadn't discovered his condition, and without his ICD, he may not still be with us.

We also shared the news that we had partnered with State Fair Community College. We were going to host heart screenings there on October 2 and 3, 2015. We screened 54 kids that weekend. This new event was two days long.

Every day we were hearing about more stories of kids with unknown heart conditions. I was learning about other heart screening foundations all over the United States. People would share stories with me on Facebook.

One story in particular really hit home with us. I reached out to the boy's mom. He was a very good high school basketball player and was already signed with Minnesota. He had collapsed on the basketball court and was saved by an AED and CPR. He was in a coma. They had implanted an ICD in his chest too.

Unfortunately for him, the college he signed with wouldn't let him play, even with parental and doctor approval. He was loyal to that team he never tried to transfer, he remained on the team just supporting his teammates. His story was on ESPN. It was very inspiring. I still keep up with his story and he even coaches basketball now.

Devon's football team did very well, and by the end of the season, he was bigger and stronger than before. He also enjoyed watching Dawson play on his first and second-grade team. That November, when Daws scored the touchdown to tie the championship game in the fourth quarter, no one cheered louder than Devon. When we scored the conversion to win it, Devon was the first one on the field to celebrate with Dawson.

I saw a glimpse of brotherly love and support. It was very touching. I know there were moments in the beginning that Devon maybe envied Dawson for being able to do the things Dev could no longer do. But as Devon's life got more normal, that faded and no one was more proud of Daws than Dev.

Thanksgiving was just around the corner, and boy did we have tons to be thankful for. There had been many close calls with Dev's health that could have gone badly. We were also thankful for all of the support for screening and the ability to help other families.

We would celebrate Christmas that year as a family and enjoy every minute of it. 2015 was one of the best and worst years of our lives. We made it through, and were ready for 2016. More sports and more doctor's appointments were coming in the new year.

31

A Better Year

OUR FAMILY PRAYED FOR A MUCH BETTER year in 2016. We had more screenings in Lincoln with Midwest Heart Check and were hoping to expand outside of Lincoln. This was going to take more work and effort, but we were up for it.

People were starting to understand the importance of heart screenings. Unfortunately I was receiving multiple messages and posts each month about kids dying suddenly from unknown heart conditions. It was very sad to hear these stories, but it motivated us even more.

Basketball went well for Devon. In March his check up appointment with Dr. T. went well too. She was impressed with his numbers, especially knowing it was during his very active basketball season. He was granted permission to continue to play basketball.

During that spring, Devon was awarded a trip from the Make-A-Wish Foundation. Devon was very excited to receive this news. The foundation was sending the four of us on a 7-day cruise. We all looked forward to the vacation very much. We would be going to Haiti, Grand Cayman, Jamaica and Cozumel.

The cruise was amazing, and we enjoyed a carefree trip with all the perks. The boys loved being able to drink all the free soda they wanted on the ship. Another great benefit was that we could go and get slices of pizza at any time of the day. Devon was able to choose one free shore excursion from the ship. He chose to swim with the dolphins in Jamaica. It was one of the most fun things we have ever done as a family. Make-A-Wish is a fabulous organization. This vacation really showed us how important these trips are to families and kids struggling with health issues, big and small.

The Fourth Annual Devon's Beat was being planned. My dad's band from Arkansas was going to perform. We also held an AED and CPR assembly at school. This was another step closer to our goal of having a heart safe school in Lincoln.

David Brader came to Lincoln to host a kicking and punting camp for local kids. It went great. It was well attended by local athletes wanting to learn more from a professional coach.

In August, we received Devon's readings from his ICD. Unfortunately, it showed he went into tachycardia for seven beats. His device was ready to kick in, but he came out of it on his own. It scared us, but his doctor reminded us this was why he had the device. His event was during rest, so it did not interfere with his activity level.

This cardiac event got to me yet again. I thanked God for our blessing of knowing about Devon's condition. This gave me another opportunity to share this with everyone to help spread awareness. I was beginning to think people might be tired of hearing from me, but decided it wasn't going to stop me.

A law was passed in 2016 requiring Missouri schools to teach CPR in Health class. Each student was required to pass it before graduation. This was very meaningful to our family.

We were able to schedule screenings in Arkansas for August 12, 2016. We were growing out of state now. I was extremely excited to host in my home state! So many of my friends from high school had the opportunity to get their kids screened. We also did a screening in Cole Camp, Missouri on November 5.

In December we received a phone call from Dr. T. Another ventricular arrhythmia was detected on Devon's device, this time six beats. There was no need for shock, Dr. T only had to increase his medication this time. Ugh! We were exhausted from this. We were still thankful he was OK, and his device was ready to work.

Two days after his episode, Dev got a surprise. He received a package in the mail. It was from Bailey Cate, the kid from Florida who kicked with Devon when he was in town visiting his grandparents.

He was a freshman punter at Old Dominion. Inside the box was a signed Old Dominion football for Devon. It said, "Keep up the hard work, the future is bright. Go Monarchs-Bailey Cate." This was very nice and such a neat surprise. A few days later Bailey was headed to the Bahamas for a bowl game.

32

Surprising Sacrifice

THE NEW YEAR STARTED OFF pretty well. Basketball was in full swing, and Dev was having a pretty good season. In February 2017, we were on the way home from a basketball game. The game did not go that great. We were all kinda hanging our heads. Not anything health-wise, just a bad loss and not Devon's best performance.

I checked my phone and had received a message on Facebook from a lady named Renae Ferguson. I knew her vaguely, because she had been a new customer at my store. The message read, "So I have a question for you! My son's birthday is coming up in a couple of weeks. Instead of him receiving gifts at his party, he was wondering if he could ask his guests for donations for your son's fundraiser?" I had tears in my eyes. I was able to change the somber conversation about losing in basketball to one about this amazing gesture.

We were speechless. It was so sweet. His name was Braeden. He was only turning seven years old. Society could learn something from kids like Braeden. He raised $180 that year! He was extremely excited to meet Devon and give the donation to him. It was such a special moment.

Devon had another episode recorded on his device. Dr. T. decided that he was simply outgrowing his medication. She made some adjustments in hopes that these issues would go away.

Unfortunately, the cardiologist for Midwest Heart Check who read the reports for our heart screenings was retiring. We were in search of another cardiologist. No one wanted to read EKGs. They only wanted to read echocardiograms. I could not agree to only having echos. The only reason we knew about Devon's condition was because of an EKG. I knew we needed those EKG's to get the proper screening.

I went to work researching heart screening organizations. While researching, I remembered a man named Eric I had connected with from Kansas. I was able to speak with his organization called My HeartCheck. We reached an agreement on working together. We scheduled our first screening with them on June 24, 2017.

They were wonderful to work with. Not only would they read the EKG's, but they did extra. They offered a little more detail to families about the screenings. Previously the family would get a report that only said, "No life threatening conditions." In addition to possible life threatening issues, My HeartCheck would give a report with more specific information. They gave a list of minor issues to keep an eye on. My HeartCheck also did all the work on their end, including the scheduling. They would send a report to the patient's family doctor too.

Summer came and went. Time seemed to be going faster. Devon was getting stronger and more consistent as a kicker. For the football preseason, the local newspaper did an article. Devon was starting his first season on the varsity as a freshman kicker. Newspaper sports reporter Johnie Logue wrote, "Their secret weapon this season is that they have a pretty good kicker in Devon Parrott. He's a freshman but will improve."

His freshman year he kicked off and did extra points only. No punting yet. The team didn't attempt a field goal until September 29, 2017. Devon made his first career high school field goal under the Friday night lights in a road game in Slater, Missouri! The crowd, players, and coaches went crazy. It was awesome! It was great to see his hard work pay off.

He went 22 for 31 with PATs and 1/1 with field goals. We won districts and came close to winning the sectional game. It was a great season.

33

Let Him Do What?

EARLY IN 2018, WE HOSTED a screening in Smithton, Missouri, a small town located 10 miles east of Sedalia. We were able to find one kid with a life threatening heart condition. He was to follow up with a cardiologist and refrain from activity until further notice. He was an athlete and his friends and family were taking it hard.

This got the attention of more Smithton families. We decided to host another event in Lincoln. Smithton was close enough for them to travel to the screenings there. Several of Dawson's baseball teammates were screened.

Daws had started on a new travel team and they were primarily Smithton kids. We shared our story with them. This helped to ensure parents would get their kids tested. It was nice to have people listen and understand the importance of getting their children screened.

One fun moment at the Lincoln screening was when Braeden got tested. He was finally of age. He had once again donated his birthday money to Devon's Beat in February and was getting tested in May. Once again it was really cool to see what this kid was doing.

I introduced Braeden to Eric and David from My HeartCheck. They shared with him how important his donations were. They were amazed at his selflessness. He was 8!

That same February, Devon attended his first national camp series with Husted Kicking in Arizona. David Brader was a coach at the camp. Dev got to meet some college and professional kickers. One he really enjoyed getting lessons from was Jason Myers. He was with the Seattle Seahawks at the time. He was later traded to the New York Jets, then back to the Seahawks. We were excited to follow his journey.

It was a long beautiful drive and a great experience. Devon even won some awards, including punting. He was becoming a stronger punter. His work ethic always impressed me. We were looking forward to the summer, Devon could get involved in more showcases for kicking and punting. He kept working to get better every single day.

The end of March came and it was time for Dev's first high school golf tournament. He had been practicing hard, but felt like he was not ready. As I was dropping him off that day, I could tell he was nervous about the tournament. I did not really know what to say because I was terrible at golf. I finally just blurted out, "Don't Suck!" He looked at me and said, "Well, I probably will because I am not very good yet." I responded, "If you do your best, we will be proud no matter what." This would become my mantra for my kids in everything they would do from that day forward. I have told or texted both of them every sporting event and important thing in their lives, "Show up, do your best, and don't suck."

Unfortunately, I was having a hard time getting Devon to a lot of the kicking camps and showcases held in St. Louis. One day David Brader called and said he had an idea. He knew a family that lived in the St. Louis area who had a kid Devon's age. He said they were a great family and reminded him of us when he met them. He suggested I allow Devon to come stay with Andy and Krista Lenzen so he could attend multiple camps with Drew. Indeed they seemed fine. However, what David suggested almost sent me into panic mode.

I laughed out loud and said, "You obviously don't know me well." He said, "I knew you'd say that, but seriously they will take great care of him. You can put him on the train, and they can pick him up."

That was even more funny. I didn't even leave Devon alone at this point. He wanted me to pack Devon up, and put him on a train with a family I met once? Actually to be clear I had only met the dad once.

When I told Devon and Jason, Dev said, "You should let me!" That's all Jason needed to hear in order to force me to go through with it. I said I would not send him on a train, I'd drop him off, and pick him up over the weekend, if I felt comfortable with his family when we talked.

That next day Krista called. This was my first time talking to her. I could already tell she was nervous. She said, "I just want to write some things down, because Andy informed me Devon has a heart condition." I decided right then, she was my kind of person.

She took things seriously and took notes. I confessed to her I was not comfortable putting him on a train. Krista interrupted me and said, "Great! because I was not going to let that happen." She told David and Andy they had lost their minds, and that she would meet me halfway. Wow! I was pretty sure she was my mental twin.

Krista completely eased my mind, and I was ready to let him go. Not only did the week form a special relationship with Drew and Dev, but we gained some great friends too. Devon had a wonderful time and they spoiled him rotten. He had some great camp experiences.

We had some epic football games that fall. Dev was a sophomore. His stand out moment was on October 12, 2018. We were down 7-8 with two minutes left. We marched down the field and got it in field goal range. Devon trotted out on the field to attempt the game winning kick. I was a mess, the whole crowd was holding their breath for the sophomore kicker. Talk about nerves of steel. He nailed it! The crowd went wild! I stayed extremely calm. Just kidding, I went absolutely crazy. We won 10-8. That night I wrote something to future Devon.

This is one for our memories!

"Future Devon, you are gonna miss some major field goals and extra points in your life. You are gonna be disappointed and you will probably disappoint others. But remember these moments! You have a unique story that has led you to this, and we expect great things! Take that bad and improve, but take the good and remember why you are doing this!"

He had other moments that year, but this one was special. We won districts, then sectionals We made it to the final four. That game was crazy.

We were playing Mid Buchanan on their home field. The winner was going to the state championship game. The game was tough, both teams had stout defenses. We were winning 14-7 with Mid-Buch driving and time winding down in the 4th quarter. They scored with a few seconds on the clock. We were up by one point. The opposing coach decided to go for two to win the game. They ran a play action pass and our defense all went toward the running back. Fortunately our free safety covered the tight end and he intercepted the pass in the endzone to send us to the state championship game. The crowd went crazy!

We were set to play at Mizzou's Faurot Field for the class one state championship. The Lenzens and Coach Brader showed up to support Devon. We also had some great friends and family.

State was not the game we wanted. We were clearly out-manned by the other team. The weather was poor, raining the whole time. It was tough; but it was a great experience.

Devon had a great year. He was 50 for 55 on PAT's and 5 for 11 on field goals. The field goal percentage seemed worse than it actually was. The coaches allowed him to try some long ones when we were winning by a large margin. They wanted to give him more game experience in case he needed to attempt a long one later in the year. He had 65 points total for the year, and was named all district kicker. It was a fun season.

34

Championship Dreams

IN FEBRUARY I RESPONDED to an Instagram post made by now NY Jets pro bowl kicker, Jason Myers. I told him a little more about Devon and his story. I told him where he was now as a kicker. Late in the month, I got a message from Jason saying Dev's story had won a contest. He mailed Devon a signed cleat he wore in the pro bowl game. It was pretty neat.

We attended another national camp series in Arizona and it was a great time. Once again Devon did fantastic. He was able to work with more collegiate and professional kickers and punters.

We hosted a screening in Stover, Missouri, in March. Krista drove three hours from St. Louis to have Drew and her other son Carter tested. She was very interested in Devon's story and was anxious to get her boys tested. Thankfully, their screenings came back clear.

Devon's Beat was great and it was extra special because the Lenzen family drove all the way to Lincoln in support of Devon. Drew and Carter both ran. I was excited to have them there.

While the race was going on, Krista told me that Drew told her he was going to win. Not just his age group, but the whole thing. He wanted to make Devon proud. He did! I couldn't believe it. That made the event more special. They also donated $500 toward Devon's beat!

The 2019 football season went great. Devon was a junior and was now kicking and punting for the team. The team went undefeated throughout the regular season. As a matter of fact, they did not even have any close games. They averaged 47 points a game and only gave up an average of nine points per game.

In the first round of the playoffs, the opposing team forfeited. The second round they played the rival Cole Camp and beat them. The district championship was the third round, where they defeated Skyline. In the quarterfinals they defeated Windsor 36-6. For the semifinal round of the playoffs they were able to host Marceline at home. They beat them 46-20 to advance to the state championship.

The state championship game was once again to be held at Faurot Field on the Mizzou campus. The opponent was the Valle Catholic Warriors. Dev was nervous, but excited for another opportunity to play for a state championship. The Lenzen's came again to support the team. The game went back and forth. In the end we had a chance to pull it out, but once again we fell short.

Devon was disappointed not to win the state championship, but he had a great season. He was an all district and all conference kicker. He had 81 points for the year. He was 75 of 82 on PAT's and two for four on field goals. He was named player of the game several times by the online high school sports website, Max Prep. He kicked off and also booted 20 punts. This team did not have to punt the ball very many times.

For the most part, 2019 was a great year. Devon was on the fast track to landing a spot on a college roster. We had no idea what was about to happen in the upcoming months. We were ready to see how the future would unfold.

35

In Loving Memory

THE YEAR STARTED OFF GREAT. We had our date officially picked out for our Eighth Annual Devon's Beat weekend. It was set for April third and fourth. Something big was in the works. We officially had a date set for our heart screenings in Thayer, Missouri.

Thayer is a town that is about 30 minutes north of Agnos, Arkansas, where I was raised and graduated from high school. I had several friends who had children that were going to Thayer to be screened.

This particular screening was extremely important to me. It was to be done in memory of Coach Bryan Tate. Coach Tate, an alumni of Thayer, was an assistant coach. He loved football. He had two brothers, one was on his high school team and the other was a long snapper and tight end for Quincy University.

Coach Tate traveled with his family every Saturday to watch his brother play college football. On one of those road trips, while in the back seat listening to music and working on a playlist, he had a cardiac event.

His parents said he made some weird noises like snoring. They immediately headed to the hospital. As they headed to the hospital, he started to turn blue. They pulled over and tried to revive him using CPR. When the ambulance arrived they took over CPR, and transported him to the hospital. Unfortunately they were not able to save him.

Coach Tate died of an unknown treatable heart condition. Friends from Thayer had shared his story with me. I knew that we needed to get screenings to Thayer to honor Coach Tate.

I reached out to the family after time had passed. They were very happy to bring Devon's Beat heart screenings to Thayer in honor of Coach Tate. His family wanted to help save young lives, and to get his brothers screened. We set the date for April 11, 2020. The year was looking to be a great one.

36

The First Episodes

ON JANUARY 27, I got a phone call from Dr. T. She had received a transmission from Devon's home device. It had recorded four tachycardia episodes since December 11. She was uncomfortable waiting until his February appointment and requested we come in the next day.

Unfortunately, the episodes were very random, with no patterns. This made it hard to know what was going on. The doctors thought maybe a lead was going bad, and Devon would need a new device. After further testing with the Boston Scientific team, they didn't find any concrete evidence of that being the problem. They should know, being the manufacturer of the device.

The next thing to try was increasing his beta blocker. Because they increased his Mexiletine the previous year to help stabilize his heartbeat in arrhythmia, this might help. We just had to be careful that it was not too much. Our job was to watch Devon for five to seven days to make sure he wasn't too lethargic. He was going to experience some tiredness and brain fog. The fatigue just did not need to continue after seven days.

Devon had been having more fast and erratic heartbeats (SVT) and extra heartbeats (PVC), which was causing more problems with his QTc intervals. This caused some concern.

Two of the SVT episodes were pretty insignificant while he was being active. One episode was accompanied by some lead "noise." That one was in English class. The most significant one was bad enough to charge his ICD. It was ready to shock him, until he came out of it on his own. This event happened when he was at home. Now we had to wait and see, and then go back sooner than we intended too.

There were other, more complicated, procedures that may or may not help type 3 Long QT syndrome. We were not ready to discuss those yet because of their speculative nature. Dr. T. advised that we would approach them if necessary. For the time being we just kept a close eye on him.

Given everything we had been through, I could not help but think; how can we be so blessed to have this kid with us? How were we blessed to know about his condition and to have this life saving device tell us when something is wrong? God definitely had a plan.

Does this suck? Absolutely! I could've thrown us a pity party at least once a month. One of his precious nurses put it this way. "He's got something pretty special in his chest that is literally a life saver. He has to live life to the fullest and is protected by his device!"

Devon told all of his doctors and nurses he was in a hurry to get back for a basketball game. They all wished him luck. There were questions about Devon having problems when active versus inactive, it's not that simple. Sports didn't cause his issues. His medical team did not let him stop living his life. We just needed to get over this most recent hurdle, or go around it.

Could he have had an episode or problem while he's active? Absolutely! The chances are higher when he's asleep in bed. It's just the type of Long QT syndrome he has. Nothing he could do athletically would cause it to be worse.

37

COVID 19

THE FIRST FEW DAYS OF A HIGH DOSE of medicine was a little rough, his beta blocker lowered his heart rate and made him lethargic, but he managed well. He was only a little tired. Dev continued to play basketball and participate in physical fitness with little to no problems. He was playing well and seemed to be handling the medication and activity well.

I think once he got out there doing what he loved, the adrenaline kicked in. He was just playing ball. Devon was really coming along and playing with fire in his eyes. He was living life to the fullest. I loved his passion for the sport.

Devon's Beat was still moving along as planned. We had donations coming in every day. I felt like it was going to be a big year. It was exciting to see what was going to come in next.

At the end of February, first of March there was talk of a new very dangerous virus that was spreading all over the World. COVID 19 was spreading fast. It was wreaking havoc on America. It was killing thousands of people and slowly the government was shutting businesses down.

In March, when the kids had spring break, they never returned to school. They were out for the rest of that school year. No sports, no classes, nothing. Everything was canceled. They did some online classes and homework, but we couldn't even have graduation. The restaurants could only have pick-up orders. It was sad to see all of the struggling businesses.

We were obviously scared for any of us to get COVID, but especially Devon. Any sickness could really affect his heart and we were afraid. I was also informed with all of the closures, I had to reschedule Devon's Beat. That was a bummer.

On March 14, It appeared the ICD lead was sensing "noise," and that could be a first sign of the device or the lead malfunction . This could be dangerous as it could lead to inappropriate shocks, or shocking the patient during the normal rhythm. We were looking into where he was during the event.

Due to the dangers of the virus, they decided to adjust his ICD to be less sensitive to certain "noise." Dr. T. consulted with another specialist. The medical team changed the settings hoping it would help the incorrect transmissions.

He was originally set to be shocked at 200 bpm. They raised it to 240 bpm. The decision was also made to change the device from one second to initiate shock to ten seconds. In addition, the team set the ICD to transmit information every two weeks, instead of every month. These changes allowed the device to know if it was a real event or not. This frightened me, but I had to trust them.

If the COVID lockdown circumstances were different, Dev would have been getting a new device sooner rather than later. However, if the urgency could wait, they were looking at the end of May or first of June for the ICD replacement.

A phone call from the doctor's office came again on March 17, 2000. They needed to push Devon's appointment up. He was having more transmissions that were not good. While they were trying not to see patients during the COVID lockdown, Dr. T. was adamant he needed to be seen sooner rather than later. We were very nervous and anxious.

On March 20, we headed to Children's Mercy to see what they had to say. It was a long morning. We had tons of information to absorb. I had more research to do. I needed to try to get my brain wrapped around everything the doctors were telling me.

There was discussion about the type of ICD to use. He could receive the same type of transvenous device or a new type of device that would be subcutaneous, underneath all layers of his skin.

The only news Devon heard was that if he was approved for a subcutaneous ICD, it would be placed in his side. This meant he would no longer have arm restrictions. He would be able to do push ups, pull ups, and bench press. He was ready to immediately sign on the dotted line.

The original device Dev had was transvenous. Which means it goes through the vein and into the heart. The subcutaneous device would be on his side under the skin, up through his chest, and around the heart. If his heart could tolerate this, it would be better for him long term.

We had to look at the risks, and make sure he could live without the pacing part of the original transvenous ICD. That was the only downside to the subcutaneous ICD. The transvenous ICD was also a pacemaker.

We would weigh the pros and cons and make decisions based on all of it. Regardless of the type, a new device was needed! We were not ready to think about him having surgery again, but ready to know what device he needed and when his surgery would take place.

38

Adapt and Move Forward

OUR COMMITTEE HAD TO MOVE Devon's Beat to May first, and second, and I was not happy about that. It was the first time I had to reschedule the event. On April 3, the day we were supposed to have Devon's Beat, I was anxious. I was waiting for Devon's device interrogation to go through. I would panic every time my phone rang. We were waiting to see if he could wait until this virus was over to get a new device, or if it would become an "emergency!"

Dev, Daws, and I were packing up schoolwork to go drop off, since our school was closed. I was constantly watching the news to see how bad the COVID virus had gotten. I wanted to know how close it was to home. I was just praying my kids didn't get it. I researched how it could affect Devon.

I got the call from Dr. T. around noon. Devon had two small episodes a few days before. These were not bad, but were within two hours of each other. She once again had discussed Devon's situation with a colleague.

Both doctors agreed, Devon needed a new device. His transvenous wire was malfunctioning. They were going to have to replace the entire device; however, they were unable to schedule due to the COVID 19 virus. The replacement could only be scheduled if it was an emergency situation, which we did not want!

I worried that there were too many episodes too quickly. Dr. T. was monitoring him closely. We were thankful for her diligence, no matter how scary it seemed.

Meanwhile things were getting worse with COVID in Missouri. I had to reschedule Devon's Beat, again. We also had to reschedule the Thayer heart screenings.

The day came to send another device transmission. It was a long Friday, April 17. We tried to send the device readings and they would not go through. We assumed we had phone troubles.

I drove Devon and his home device in town to try and send it. We tried to send it from my work, Johnson Tax Service. No luck. We went to Shelter Insurance, where LeeAnn works. Nothing. Off we went to our friend Betty's house, and still nothing.

Turns out, after hours of trying and being on the phone, that the at-home device was also malfunctioning. Both devices malfunctioned! Ugh! As you can imagine, it was very frustrating and nerve-racking.

They had to expedite a new machine, and we were back to waiting again. Boston Scientific got the device to us quickly. Once again we got more bad news. Three more "noise" events. The device was toast, but still not considered an emergency surgery.

If COVID had not existed, we would have had a new device already. This year was not going well, but we held on to the fact that Devon was with us. Thankfully, we were all relatively healthy.

The new dates for Devon's Beat were set for June 12, and 13. We were moving forward, praying every day would be a good day.

39

Fractured

AT 1:40 P.M. on April 27, 2020, I got a phone call from Dr. T. She was talking super fast, I could barely understand her. Devon's lead wire had fractured. We had to get him to the hospital as soon as possible.

The device needed to be turned off before it shocked him inappropriately. Even though his heart was fine, the fractured wire made it appear to be a medical emergency. The device could shock him while he was alert and awake. Dr. T. said this would feel like a horse kicked him in the chest. This would not be a good situation.

She was very concerned about him not having a working device and wanted it replaced. No one at Children's Mercy would be available to assist Dr. T. in the surgery because of COVID. She was searching for alternatives.

She had contactedThe University of Kansas Medical Center to see if anyone there could perform an ICD removal and then place the new device. KU medical agreed to perform the surgeries. We packed our bags, called Jason, and headed to KU Medical Center.

Going to KU made me nervous. It was new territory for us. Dr. T. assured us she would be there and scrub in to assist with his surgery. We got to KU and were informed that Devon would be admitted. They would shut off his device for safety. The staff assured us they would have him hooked up to monitors in case of cardiac arrest. In addition, AED pads would be placed on him just in case.

It was just Devon and me for the initial appointment, and I could not shake this terrible feeling. They explained he would have a lead wire and ICD extraction. If that surgery went well, they would also implant his new device. They had a heart surgeon on call and available for any medical emergencies.

As with any surgery, they explained all of the risks. This is when I got the worst feeling. The KU doctor listed all of the things that could go wrong. Most of them are not that big of a deal. Then they told me if the lead wire is embedded in the vein it is a problem. If they don't know it in time, it can rip and cause it to bleed. The blood could go into the heart chamber, and it could stop his heart.

The doctor explained there is a three percent chance of this happening, but that they always have procedures in place in case it does. They would go in, scope the heart, and see what was going on. The heart surgeon would be called in to fix it. The heart surgeon is required to be within seven minutes of the OR at all times.

I was frozen. I tried to stay brave for Devon, who took those words with a grain of salt. He was a little worried and scared for this surgery, but was looking forward to this drama being over. He was anxious for his new device that would free up even more of his previous restrictions.

I just couldn't get it off my mind. All I could think about was the worst possible scenario happening. To top things off, there was a question as to whether I could even stay at the hospital with him because of COVID. One of the surgeons informed me they had no intentions of kicking me out, since he was under 18. It was a good thing. That was going to be a fight I believe I would have won!

I called Jason. He was on his way to KU Medical Center after making sure Dawson was safe at a friend's house. I told Jason what the doctor said. While he was also worried, he was much stronger than me. He assured me everything was going to be fine.

I hardly slept. I could not shake that awful feeling. It had consumed me, but I tried to keep it to myself. I did text a friend or two my fears, but tried to suppress them. I was very frustrated that I couldn't shake the feeling. The reason I was frustrated came to me in the middle of the night.

A few years after Devon's diagnosis, I saw an email from SADS expressing thoughts and prayers for a SADS family. I read that their son had passed away the day before. I messaged my contact at SADS. I knew they couldn't tell me everything, but asked what had happened. He was a LQTS patient with an ICD. She messaged me back. He had a rare complication during a routine ICD extraction.

That memory came flooding back to me. I remembered reading her message and being scared knowing one day Devon would need a new device. My contact told me it was very rare, and not to worry. There I sat April 27, 2020, remembering that kid's story and praying it wouldn't happen to Devon. I decided I was overreacting and tried to sleep. Tried!

40

Surgery

THE NEXT MORNING the team came to take Devon to surgery prep. The nurse wheeled him back to his room and dropped us by the waiting room. They informed us that once he was prepped we could be with him until surgery.

Once again it was a little different because of COVID. Most people could only have one person in the waiting room and no one could go back once they went to prep. Because he was a minor, they allowed both Jason and me to be there. Thank God! I could not do any of this alone.

It took forever for them to prep him for surgery. I went to the nurses station and asked, "Can I see him yet?" On the third time I got hysterical. I was afraid they were going to send him to surgery without us getting to see him, hug him, tell him we loved him. I could not imagine not getting to say and do those things.

I was trying not to think,"What if it's the last time?" By then, I was slowly losing it. The nurse's station attendant was very understanding and was about in tears as I was begging to see Devon. She called his prep nurses and said I was visibly upset and needed to see him. They assured her he was about ready and would call us in soon. I was shaking and weak, but pulled myself together. They finally called us back.

There Dev was just as cool as a cucumber. It gave me calming joy to see him relaxed and eager to get the surgery started. Although my gut was in knots, it made me realize I was overreacting. If he could be calm and positive, so could I. Jason was nervous, but he was calm. Like always, he only saw the good side of things.

Jason and I were able to spend almost an hour with Dev. They came in to take him back, and went over the risks of surgery again. My heart was pounding, and my eyes were tearing up. Jason assured me he would be fine. Devon himself told me it was all good. I got my hug and kiss and we told him how much we loved him. Then, they wheeled him away.

I just sat in the surgical prep area and cried. This was by far the scariest moment in my life. The hospital staff told us if everything went OK, they would be in surgery for about four hours. This was going to be a long wait.

The nurse would check in from time to time to let us know how things were going. We would get an update when the surgical team had the ICD wire extracted. After that, they would start the implantation of the new device. No big deal right?

We went to the waiting room and I was very uneasy. Jason kept assuring me everything was going to be fine. We talked about how excited Devon was to get his new device. The device that would allow him to do things he hadn't been able to do in seven years. Push-ups, pull-ups, and bench press were on the top of his list.

The hospital seemed like a ghost town. Very few people were in the waiting area, and everyone was wearing masks. COVID was everywhere by that point. Everyone was very fearful of the virus.

I just sat, stared off into space, and got very emotional. I tried to distract myself by texting people. I let them know that they had started Devon's surgery. I thanked them for their thoughts and prayers.

All of a sudden it hit me. I had received a message via facebook from Candice Fowler, a friend from Lincoln, the night before. She had seen my post, and wanted to check on Devon. She had asked me if she could call and pray with us that night.

This was sent to me in the chaos of Devon being checked in, me hearing the risks of the surgery, the team turning off his ICD, and the doctors assuring me he would be safe.

I saw the message. I told myself I'd respond later. When later came, Jason arrived, and more doctor and nurse stuff happened. I was not thinking about the message. Although I was struggling with the thought of the events for the next day, I put this message on the back burner. I knew she would understand.

I finally messaged her back. I told her it was getting late, and asked if we could do it tomorrow. She informed me she would be praying for us. She said she would reach out after her own medical procedure she'd be having that day.

I felt guilty! Why didn't I just let her call me at any time? It should be OK for a friend to call me at any time.

Now, I know why. I believe in God. I believe in all the things possible through prayer. However, anything religious made me uncomfortable. I did not want her to feel obligated to call and pray with us. I didn't talk about it much at all. I have said my prayers through the years, but it was not something I spoke of much.

I felt terrible. I was basically making excuses not to let her call and pray with us. There was too much going on. It was too late. She didn't care, she was there when I was ready. Feeling uneasy sitting in the waiting room, I asked myself, "Why didn't I call her?" I need it now more than ever. But now she was busy with her own medical problem.

Finally, they came out and said, "Sorry, we had a slow start, but he is doing fine." This was about two hours after they had taken him back to start the surgery. Jason and I were glad to hear the positive report.

There was a moment when Whiteman Air Force Base did a flyover. It was a scheduled flyover to honor those who lost their lives to COVID 19. It was overwhelming! I remember telling Jason, "Wow! Dev is big stuff, he got a flyover." I was smiling, but my heart was pounding. It felt very weird.

41

Can't Shake This Feeling

EVERYTHING FELT WEIRD. Jason could tell I was slowly losing it. He thought it was time to get up and move. Time to go look around and people watch.

We walked down to the cafeteria and got a snack to bring back. I was looking at my watch and told him we should have an update by now. It was almost 1 p.m., and we needed to head back to the waiting room for a report.

While on our way back to the waiting room, I spotted Devon's prep nurses going to lunch. Wait, what? They told me they would be waiting in his recovery room until he came back. I told Jason, "I think we missed an update. Why are the nurses going to lunch?"

We got back to the waiting room and nothing. I was starting to feel better. I just couldn't understand why they didn't give us another update.

Around 2 p.m., a lady came running into the waiting room, just like in the movies, yelling "PARENTS OF DEVON PARROTT?" We were startled at first. But as soon as I realized it, I knew something was very wrong. Everyone in the waiting room was looking at us with sorrow. The nurse, with fear and regret in her eyes, said it all. I was on the verge of losing it.

They ushered us to a private space, which happened to be the entrance to the hospital chapel. I was confused, but was I? I actually knew what they were going to say. But the words were not easy to take in.

The nurse was hysterical. While she is human, she should have been better prepared to talk to Jason and me . The situation could have been handled much differently.

Devon had encountered serious complications and he bled out. They had to call in the heart surgeon, who was with him now. The surgeon had to crack his chest and fix the problem. Devon was on heart bypass. The medical team had no idea if he would make it or not.

I fell to my knees and sobbed, "You have to help him! You have to save him! I cannot lose him!" My exact fears seemed to be coming true. The heavy weight of this awful news was crushing me.

There was terror in the nurse's eyes. Jason picked me up off of the floor and told me, "Devon is a fighter. He will be OK." Jason basically carried me to the waiting room next door. I can't even remember going to that room. But I can remember begging out loud to no one in particular, "Please help Devon!"

Dr. T. finally came out and started explaining to us what had happened. She said she was very sorry for the complication during the extraction. The heart surgeon needed to step in emergently and stabilized Devon. She was literally pumping his heart with her hands to keep the oxygen going to his brain.

The KU doctor came in and apologized for the situation that had happened. I could not even listen to him. I was very angry! We were extremely scared. Our world was crashing down around us.

The emergency heart surgeon finally got him stable. We had to wait, not so patiently, until the nurses had Devon ready in the ICU. This took hours. I have no real memory of the exact timeline, but it seemed like an eternity.

The doctors and nurses would pass by looking at us. They looked at us with such sorrow on their faces. I asked Jason why they kept looking at me like that. Why weren't they letting us see him, or telling us he is better?

I was hysterical by then. I was begging for Devon to be OK. I told Jason, I could not go on without Devon. I cried in the bathroom. I needed him to be alive and I begged God to bring him back. I just wanted him alive. I needed him, we needed him! I convinced myself he was going to wake up. He had to. Then I would just start sobbing. He had to, we could not go on without him.

I just could not imagine what to do or say without him. I thought of all the things he had been through. He was helping save the lives of others through Devon's Beat. What would I do with Devon's Beat? I could not keep it going without him. I would hate cancelling it, but would not be able to do it if he was gone.

Dr. T. checked on us several times. She just held me while I cried. She told me she was very sorry. Had she known it was going to be like this, she would have done it all differently. It was several hours of waiting to see him.

Many people were texting, messaging, and calling me to check on Devon. They all knew way too much time had passed. We sent vague messages about Devon. We didn't want anyone reaching out to Dawson; he didn't know yet. I didn't know what to tell him. I had no idea how to explain what was going on and how I was feeling.

42

ICU

AFTER SEVERAL HOURS, we finally got to see Devon. They warned us that seeing him was going to be scary. Let me tell you, when they warn you, the warning doesn't prepare you for what he actually looked like. It was hard to see.

The doctors told us he was doing OK. At least he was alive. He was at risk for brain injury due to loss of oxygen during his cardiac event.

When he coded on the operating table, they performed CPR. It was unknown how his body would handle the oxygen loss. We had to wait and see. Devon was in a coma and the ventilator was breathing for him.

The Doctors told us exactly what went wrong. Our hearts are protected by a thin outer lining called the pericardium. It is like a sac around the heart. The doctor began extracting the lead wire from the vein via scope. Suddenly, his heart stopped beating. Devon coded. They had no idea why until quickly putting a camera in the scope to see what was going on. Devon's pericardium was full of blood. Immediately they knew they had torn his vein while extracting the wire.

At that point the on-call heart surgeon was notified. It took several minutes for him to come and the doctors and nurses took turns doing chest compressions on Devon to keep the blood supply flowing.

Once the heart surgeon finally arrived, he performed a sternotomy to crack his chest open. He immediately began repairing the tear. His goal was to get in and out as quickly as possible, repairing the tear and closing him up.

Not everyone in the operating room agreed with the choice to close him up ASAP. The surgeon said it was too much trauma for his body, they had to get him closed up. While he was repairing the tear, other doctors and nurses were literally massaging Devon's heart to keep blood flowing.

They had to abort the device removal procedure. Dev still had the wire from his ICD in his chest and did not have his new device.

When I saw him, I tried to stay calm and strong. That was tough! I thought about the percentages. Last night and earlier that morning, we were told that this was a routine surgery and that there was only a three percent chance of this happening. THREE PERCENT! Here we were living that three percent chance.

My initial prayer was answered. He was alive. The doctors told us the next 24/48 hours were critical. Devon needed to make small improvements. He needed to follow commands. He needed to know his name. The slightest movements on his own would be positive.

We got to stay with him for a while. I was praying for anything and everything. I was begging him to open his eyes. He did open them once. Dev didn't know it, but I saw his eyes. I thanked God. He also made some involuntary movements, they weren't much, but they were something. Again, I thanked God!

Time came for the ICU shift change and we got kicked out about 7 p.m. I didn't want to go. I was lost and scared. I was still thankful Devon opened his eyes and made a few twitches.

43

Hard Calls

WE WENT TO THE ICU waiting room. Jason and I decided it was time to make some very difficult phone calls. I went to the bathroom first, just to be alone. I cried my eyes out. I told Jason I just needed to freshen up. I really just went in there to lose it, alone.

I decided to look at my facebook to see if anyone was asking tons of questions. I had a message from Candace Fowler, she videoed herself saying a prayer for Devon. Even though I had not been able to connect with her by phone, she took the time to lift us up in prayer.

My heart, which was extremely heavy, somehow felt lighter. This weird calming feeling came over me as I watched and listened to her prayer video. I thought, "God and Devon got this. There is no way I am losing Devon tonight."

I heard a knock at the door and it was Jason, "Ang are you OK?" I realized how long I had been in there. I pulled myself together and came out.

We both decided to call our parents one at a time so we could be there to support each other. It was difficult. It was extremely hard on me to call my mom and dad. I just did not know how to express all of this overwhelming emotion.

I felt like a failure. I felt weak and negative. I couldn't pull myself together and be strong. What was wrong with me? Devon is in there being a hero and fighting for his life and I was an absolute mess.

Hearing strong, tough Jason get emotional talking to his parents really got to me. Jason was very strong and positive. But, for the first time that night, I saw he was only being strong for me. At that moment, I realized I needed to try harder to be strong for him too. I am not sure I ever accomplished that, but I tried.

While on the phone, I discovered I had tons of text messages. Lots of thoughts and prayers and checking in. Many asked, "What do you need? I'll be there as soon as I can." But, two messages back-to-back just brought me a world of hope!

My good friend Becky Schenewark and my friend and coworker Ashley Pilant both sent me a picture of a double rainbow that was seen in Lincoln. They both texted. First, "We have a double rainbow over Lincoln tonight. I know this is God watching over Devon." The other said, "God is letting all of us know Dev is going to be OK."

I pulled myself together again. I said, "This isn't over, Devon is too strong." I decided to pray again. This time I thanked God that Devon was alive and for letting me see his eyes.

While I told God I wasn't trying to be selfish, I prayed for him to do the next steps for us. *Please let him follow small commands, like squeeze my hand and open his eyes. Please! God!*

44

Small Steps

WE FINALLY GOT BACK in the ICU around 9 p.m. and had another visit with the doctors. They were pleased with his involuntary moments and hopeful it was trending in the right direction. This was still a waiting game.

We said, "Devon, if you can hear us, please open your eyes. We need to see your eyes." He did! I asked if he was OK and he nodded his head! Oh my heart! I cried tears of joy! The nurses were pleased. They talked to the doctor and were going to start weaning him off the ventilator. Once again, I was thanking God!

Around 12 a.m. on April 29, 2020, we asked Devon to squeeze our hands, and he did! The respiratory therapist decided to do a breathing test on him. This would tell them more about his progress.

The test startled him. Dev was becoming more conscious. He did not like the breathing tube. He was fighting it and scaring me. He was still relying on it to help him breathe, but he was trying to get it out.

He hated it and was becoming agitated. The nurses called the doctor and he came in. The doctor said, "The boy wants to breathe on his own; let's let him!"

I had to leave the room while they extubated him. I was glad I left the room. One because I can't watch that kind of thing. Secondly, I was afraid he wouldn't be able to breathe on his own. I was nervous he would code again. I could not see that. It was hard enough to see him with tubes and probes everywhere. I don't think I could see him being brought back to life.

Once they removed the tube, he calmed down. He was out of it again, which made me sad. Even though we were making progress, I wanted him to wake up.

The nurses explained to us that all of his progress was great. We would know if there was brain damage when he could wake up and tell us his name. There were still plenty of hurdles to jump.

Being patient was getting difficult. I was wanting things to progress faster. I went back to praying.

" Dear God, thank you so much for bringing Devon back to us. I am eternally grateful. I'm trying not to ask for too much. I want to ask for Devon to know who he is. Please let him wake up and know who he is, who we are. If not, I trust you and will forever be grateful just to have him alive."

45

There He Is!

IT WAS GETTING TO BE EARLY in the morning near the 1:00 hour. They told us, because of COVID, one of us had to leave. Jason didn't even question it. He knew I could not leave. While he didn't want to go, he knew he'd just be a few blocks away at the hotel. He never once asked me to leave instead. He just knew. He needed his rest too.

Devon was breathing on his own and taking small commands. The nurses and I kept bothering Devon throughout the night and into the early morning. He was well taken care of.

At one point he woke up. I said "Devon, do you know who I am? I am your mom and I love you very much Devon. You are doing so good." He looked at me with a blank stare. Dev was scared and confused.

When he closed his eyes again, I completely lost it. I cried my eyes out. He didn't know me. He didn't know what was going on or who I was. I pulled it together and remembered I promised I would not be disappointed, only grateful he was alive.

Around 2 a.m., the doctors came in and pestered him again. This time he was more alert. The doctor asked him his name. He looked scared and confused.

He looked at me like please help me. I said "Devon you have to listen to him." He got agitated, like why are they waking me up and asking me this? I said, "Devon stop being difficult, you have to answer him. Tell him your name." He would not even look at the doctor and angrily answered, "It's DEVON!"

The doctor, who was in tears, responded, "There he is. Devon, glad to have you back. Can you tell me who this lady is beside you?" Once again he looked at me very angry. I said, "Do you know who I am?" Without looking at the doctor again he said, "My mother!" I had tears of joy streaming down my face and I couldn't text Jason fast enough.

Devon was alive and could move on command. Not only that, he knew his name. He also knew I was his mom! That was the best feeling I could have at that moment.

Jason was at the hospital really early the next morning. He wanted to see for himself. When he got there, the doctor was already back in the room.

The doctor was amazed at his progress and very thankful. He ran Devon through all of the tests of "who are you?" and "who is this?"

When Jason walked in, the doctor said, "Who is this guy?" Devon said, "I have no idea I have never seen him a day in my life." Then Devon smiled from ear to ear and said, "Just kidding, it's my dad." That even got Dad a little teared up.

Dev was alive, he knew who we were, and he could even crack a joke. He was in and out that morning, but when he was awake he would talk to us.

Jason quizzed him every time he woke up. He knew what month it was. Devon also knew his brother's name and who his cousins were.

As the day moved on, he got poked and prodded. Devon had his chest tube, sheath, and unnecessary IV's removed. He was not amused, but was looking more like himself every minute.

That afternoon, the nurses sat him in a chair. That's when we noticed his motor skills were not normal. Dev could not use his hands very well to grab ahold of things. I kind of freaked out, but the nurses assured me it was normal. Therapy would help him regain motor function. I was pretty upset thinking he may not be able to function normally. I had to remind myself to not be greedy. He was alive.

They let him eat normal food. He ordered the chicken parmesan and a brownie. Dev seemed to enjoy being able to eat. It was the little things in life at that stage of the process.

Meanwhile, some of my sweet friends ordered Jason and me pizza delivery. It was much needed and appreciated. Many people were very willing to help.

We soon learned his short-term memory was not good. As soon as he had eaten, his nurse came in and said, "Oh you ate. What was for lunch?" He told her pizza and cinnamon sticks, which it most certainly was not. We decided to quiz him more. We discovered his short-term memory was gone.

We told him he ate chicken parm and a brownie. He said, "Oh yeah, duh." Then we would wait 5-10 minutes and ask what he had for lunch. It was pizza and cinnamon sticks again. This carried on all day and night. I was getting concerned. Again, I prayed.

46

13 Minutes

DEVON WAS ALLOWED TO GET UP and walk the hall. I was proud to see him walking. It was a huge relief after seeing his motor skills weren't great.

Throughout the day, almost every doctor or nurse on his team came to see him. He was a miracle. They could not believe he was awake, much less talking and walking.

Many staff members told us they prayed for him and went home with heavy hearts awaiting any good news. They were really invested in his case. We could tell they cared deeply about their patients.

His ICU nurse told me she called her mom and said, "I can't tell you any information, but can you please put this young boy on your prayer chain at church?" Her mother gladly agreed to do that.

I was telling her I was overwhelmed with everyone on Devon's medical team's response. I confessed to her that I realized things in the operating room must have been even worse than I imagined. Thank God I didn't know that while I was in the waiting room.

She said, "I don't know of anyone that has ever coded for 13 minutes, and was not only alive but walking and talking. To top that off, he knows who he is."

I said, "Wait what? 13 minutes?" Even I know, people don't survive after coding for 13 minutes. Her eyes filled with fear, and she said, "Oh my goodness, I thought you knew that. I am very sorry."

Jason was gone at that moment, and Devon was asleep. I stood staring out the window, I was very thankful to have Devon. However, I was very angry to just now hear that news.

I was not angry with the nurse; she genuinely thought I knew. I was angry that I didn't know sooner. It made me wonder what actually happened. What took so long to revive him?

I just stood there and cried. She came in again and apologized. I simply thanked her. She had given me even more evidence that we had witnessed a true miracle. God used Devon's strength and the fight the surgeon insisted on bringing to the operating table to perform a miracle.

The shift nurse came in bearing great news. After only 24 hours, Devon was ditching the ICU and headed to a regular room. This was a great step in the right direction.

Before we left, I started realizing the medical team of the hospital had made some type of mistake. Slowly, people from the administration of the hospital were coming into the room to check on Devon.

They all seemed uneasy and very apologetic. They were offering to pay for hotel stays, meals, and wondering what they could do to make it easier on us.

At the time, I was overwhelmed with gratitude that they saved my kid. I wasn't exactly picking up on their fears. But they were definitely there. There was something they were not telling us.

One of the ICU doctors we loved told us that the upper administration, from the top floor, had demanded that Jason and I not be in the ICU because of COVID. The ICU doctor told them,

"This is a child, their child. They have endured a vast amount of trauma today. We don't even know for sure if their child will wake up. I will not ask them to leave. If you want them to leave you go tell them, but I promise you, it will not go well."

Needless to say, he did not try to kick us out of the ICU. We were able to witness Devon's great improvements over the course of the day. Jason and I were very glad to be moving Devon to a regular room.

47

New Digs

GETTING HIM SETTLED IN and learning the ins and outs of the new floor took time. Devon was exhausted, and still a little groggy. Unfortunately, he was not fully comprehending everything that was going on.

Once again we were surrounded by cute, sweet nurses who already knew about Devon. They were amazed by his progress. He was the talk of the floor. Everybody loves to hear about a miracle.

Once we got him settled and he was resting, I sat over in the corner. I went through the last day and a half in my mind. It was overwhelming as I was looking through texts and messages and posts all made for Devon. Some were made even before anyone knew what was going on—Pictures of friends and family sending prayers and well wishes. My friend Ashley took everyone at work a Devon's Beat shirt to wear the day of his surgery and they sent me a picture with prayers!

I was crying about how close we were to losing him, but also at how happy I was to have him alive. It was hard to see him struggling with memory loss and poor motor skills. I was glad to see he knew everything about his life before surgery.

I was crying because I was overwhelmed by the fact that I knew we witnessed a miracle. We witnessed a strong kid overcome something horrific. I had never seen anything like this. The odds were against him, but with God's help he prevailed.

After Devon was out of danger, Jason convinced me to go to the hotel. I needed a shower, and just to get out of the hospital. I will never forget the contrasting emotions I felt that morning on the walk from and back to the hospital.

The walk to the hotel was awful. I was riddled with fear and guilt for leaving Devon's side. I walked as fast as I could. The less time I could be gone the better . When I got to the room, I took a very quick shower.

When I had gotten dressed, I took a deep breath and started the walk back to the hospital. This time I walked slower, and I felt a breath of fresh air, literally. I felt the breeze in my hair and the sun on my face. I just stopped and looked at the sky and soaked it all in. I could feel it again, the miracle of life.

48

Hospital Woes

JASON LOOKED OVER AT ONE POINT confused trying to figure out why I was so emotional. We had our boy, and we should be feeling better. Why was I crying? I just simply said, "I don't know, I can't explain it and I can't stop it." Eventually I was able to get past all of the tears and emotional ups and downs.

That night I could tell Dev seemed a little more with it. The short term memory was still shaky. We kept asking him about his lunch and telling him exactly what he had. He still couldn't tell us five minutes later.

At dinner time, he ordered a cheeseburger and tater tots. They didn't have fries which he really wanted. Minutes after he ate, he told us he had cheese balls, a cheeseburger, and a piece of his dad's Texas toast.

Dad had no such thing, nor did he even eat in the hospital. Cheeseburger he got right, yay! Tater tots not cheese balls. Ugh! We just kept at it, and even got a few laughs at times. We felt like this couldn't be real. He had to be messing with us like when he was a kid with his colors and the M&Ms.

Before bed, after Jason left for the night, I had explained to Dev for the thousandth time that he couldn't get out of bed by himself. I also had to remind him each time he coughed, laughed, or got up, he had to use the heart shaped pillow the doctor gave him.

We had been arguing over that pillow the entire day! He could not comprehend what the pillow was for. His lack of short-term memory was not helping the situation.

Devon was starting to get a little groggy. I said, "Devon, you have to use the pillow." He looked at me with a silly look and then petted it like he was five with a stuffed animal. Then proclaimed, " I don't want it." I said, "What do you have against the pillow? The doctor and nurses said you have to use it." He said "NO!" "Devon, why do you hate the pillow?" I asked. He petted it again. It finally came to me, he did not know how he got the pillow. "Devon, where do you think this pillow came from?" I quizzed. He answered, "The gift shop?" I could hardly contain my laughter. He said, "Did granny make it?"

He thought it was a childish gift he got because he was in the hospital. He was still confused. Which brought up what had actually happened to him. Yet again, I had to tell him what happened. He could not remember the whole thing. I said, "Devon the doctor gave you this pillow to protect you. You had open heart surgery. You have a long incision on your chest." I could tell he kind of understood, but wasn't exactly getting it.

Dev was getting sleepy again, and it was time for bed. Jason had gone back to the hotel room. My high school friends had paid for the room for us. Once again an abundance of blessings were received. Many people were reaching out to offer us assistance; food, money for expenses, and hotel rooms. Our family, friends, and community know how to show up and help out.

When he finally fell asleep, so did I after I prayed again. I thanked God for our miracle, our blessing, and told him I would be content no matter what.

I wanted to pray for Devon to get that little piece of him back that he was missing. His memory! I had already told Devon about what went wrong several times. Unfortunately, it was getting harder to tell him about it each time. It was like he was hearing it for the first time every time. I did notice the last time I talked about it, he seemed to absorb it more. He also started using the pillow without me reminding him. This was another step in the right direction.

49

April 30, 2020

I WOKE UP TO DEVON NOT BEING in his bed. I freaked out! I didn't know where he was. I heard a noise in the bathroom. He had gotten out of bed and was trying to go by himself.

I busted into the bathroom and said "What are you doing?" He said, "Peeing!?" "Devon, you cannot just get up by yourself, what are you thinking!?" I exclaimed.

By then, the nurse was in there and you could tell Devon was confused. We got him back to bed. The nurse told him if he didn't want to wake me to use his call button, and she would help him.

Dev looked confused and simply said, "I can't go pee?" My heart sank. He did not remember what was going on. He was really struggling to process it all. I am sure his world seemed very out of sorts.

I had to remind him again about his surgery. The nurse could tell I was upset and struggling. She spoke up, "You can go pee Devon, we just don't want you getting out of bed by yourself just yet. Please let mom or me know." When she left, he still looked confused.

I decided to change the subject and ordered him something for breakfast. Once he was fully awake, I proceeded to tell him again about why he was in the hospital, why he had to use that lame pillow, and why he couldn't just get up and go pee.

This time it was absolutely brutal. I could tell he was scared. His eyes also showed sadness. He was worried, but he didn't ask many more questions. I still kept it vague. He simply said, "Mom they really jacked me up didn't they. It was supposed to be a simple surgery."

I texted Jason all that had happened. It wasn't long before he was there. I was praying again. Praying Devon could get his memory back, and praying he wouldn't struggle with school. He took pride in being smart and doing well in school. I did not want him to lose that.

I could handle whatever was thrown our way, but I knew Devon would have a hard time if things weren't as easy now. He kept trying to figure it all out.

Devon went for another walk that morning. He was actually more alert than the day before. Showing signs of improvements, he could tell us what he had for breakfast and get everything right..

Jason had to run back to Lincoln. He needed to check on Dawson. We were also getting low on clothes. Obviously, we had not planned on being tied down in Kansas City for more than a few days.

50

Impressive!

THE SUNDAY BEFORE DEVON'S SURGERY happened, Devon and I were discussing his dual credit class. It was just about over. All he had left was his final due Thursday, April 30! I was telling Devon and Jason that morning that I was going to email his teacher and see if he could get an extension.

I asked Jason to bring his laptop back. While Jason was gone, Devon decided he was finally ready to get his phone out. He looked at some texts he had. By some, I mean a whole lot.

Many friends, family, and all of his coaches sent texts. There was one text that got Devon to smile big, and even got some laughs out of him. Of course it would be from his best friend Bryce Koll. It was simple. Not many words, just a video from the movie "Hot Rod." The stupid movie that apparently Devon and Bryce found hilarious. It was perfect! It was the smile I had dreamed of seeing again!

Jason got back and filled me in on how Dawson was doing. I had been able to see him briefly the day before when Jason's parents brought him to the hospital. We wanted to tell him in person what had happened. I got to hug him and see that big-tooth grin that made my heart very happy.

Jason brought the computer. By then, we had decided maybe Jason could help Devon with the computer and test if needed. It was a History class and Jason was pretty good in that department. We were not the type of people to do his work for him, but thought if he had his long term memory he would be fine.

Jason broke out the laptop and was getting logged in. He was not doing it exactly right, and Devon was "back seat driving." Jason said, "It sounds to me like you know what you are doing." He gave him the laptop. Devon had one hour to take his test. Before he started his test, I just had to remind him, "Don't Suck!" In just under an hour he finished and got a 26 out of 30. That kid did it!

As Devon was submitting the test, his doctor came in. This was the doctor who performed the extraction. He said, "Hey Devon, nice to see you up and playing games on your computer. That is great for memory exercises."

I said, "He is actually submitting a final for his dual credit class that is due tonight." "What? Are you kidding me?" The doctor asked. He got a little emotional after Devon showed him he got a 26 out of 30. He said, "Kid you are something else. Yesterday we didn't even know if you would know who you were, and today you are taking a final for a college class. You do not know how happy this makes me."

I was still upset about what happened to Devon and wasn't sure exactly how it happened. I knew that the doctor was relieved not to lose a patient. He was also truly happy that Devon was going to be OK.

I think multiple doctors and nurses were pleased with their life-saving abilities, but they knew there was more to it than that. Someone was looking out for Devon. Devon was a strong resilient kid! By the way, the prayers I said earlier about Devon not struggling with school, I guess they were answered too.

51

The Life Vest

ON MAY 1, 2020, WE WOKE UP and things were looking better yet again. The surgeon who saved Devon's life, as I refer to him, came to visit. He said,

> *"Well hi Devon, I hear you were taking college finals yesterday. You had a lot of us worried, but I guess we were wrong. How would you feel about going home today or tomorrow?"*

This news was amazing. We couldn't even believe it.

We had lots of steps before he could be released, but it was now something we could look forward to. He had to get an EKG, and needed to be fitted for a life vest.

Sitting around waiting for these tests, I took a moment to update everyone. While on Facebook, I went through some of my messages and comments again. I had people from all over messaging us. It was comforting to read them again. There was a message that stood out to me. It simply read, "Hi, I know you don't know me, but I heard about your son and I have been praying." Wow! It was really comforting.

We had rival schools sending cards, messages, and even money. My boss paid me even though I couldn't be at work. A kindergarten teacher from Lincoln, Mrs. Tracey Harms, had a daughter that lived in Kansas City. She sent her daughter to check on us and she bought Devon and me lunch.

The news of Devon had spread far and wide. It was beautiful. There is no doubt it was very helpful to have everyone praying for him. One thing we had learned for sure, there is power in prayer!

We wanted to go home very badly. But when they came in to tell us about the life vest, we were not extremely happy about it. He had to wear this bra-like thing that was connected to a device that would shock him if needed.

It was awful! Since they couldn't get his device implanted, he had to have it in case of emergencies. He needed the life vest until he could get a new device. It was hideous, and he could only take it off to shower.

Like I promised God, we would take whatever we got. As long as we could take Devon home with us, we were good. We joked that he had to wear a bra for a while. This would help him understand and sympathize with what women had to go through.

Dev and I were driving on the way home together. "Mom, I know you've probably told me, but what happened exactly?" he asked. I went through the whole story again. He started asking me questions. I could tell he was finally getting it. He was getting emotional, but wanted to know more.

I told him everything, and we both cried. Stopping to catch my breath at times, I would continue. I had never told him, until that day, how scared we were that we were going to lose him forever. The doctors were convinced he wouldn't be the same. I even told him about the feelings I had and all of the prayers I had prayed. I showed him the double rainbow pictures I had received.

"Sorry for telling you too much," I said. I needed Devon to know that I felt like we were blessed. He needed to understand he was a real miracle. "I need to know, thank you for sharing everything," he said.

Dev told me something that day that both broke my heart, and made me cry tears of joy at the same time. He was glad he was crying. I didn't understand. He told me there was a time in his life he didn't know if he was capable of feeling emotional enough to cry. He felt broken. Like nothing made him cry. He remembered not even feeling sad when some bad things had happened. He wasn't happy they occurred, but he just couldn't cry about it.

I suspected this all happened when he was first diagnosed. Maybe he just turned off his emotions so he couldn't hurt anymore. He was relieved to be crying and of course we cried some more. This was a very therapeutic ride home from Kansas City.

Looking back, I thought this was one of the "everything happens for a reason" moments I have been talking about since 2012. I had that feeling again. But, I was starting to get used to it. It was an emotional week. I was bringing home my walking, talking miracle.

52

Home Sweet Home

ON FRIDAY, MAY 1, 2020, pulling into the driveway at our home literally took my breath away. There was a flood of emotions that hit me. It was the longest five day roller coaster of emotions I had ever experienced. I could not help but be both grateful and overwhelmed. I certainly hoped I would never have to ride that roller coaster again.

We had several surprises from my sweet friends. My house was cleaned by my friends Angie, Heather, and Marsha. Our yard was mowed by Devon's friends Gabe, and Levi.

My mom, dad, and Dawson were waiting for us. It was good to be home. You do not realize how much you miss the comforts of home until they are taken away.

In the hospital, there was no way I could see myself going home without Devon. I knew I had to consider that possibility. Honestly, I could not even imagine trying. I had longed for and prayed for this day. God granted us the miracle of it coming to fruition.

I apologized to Devon for crying again. Being the sweet kid he is, he told me he understood. We got in and got all the hugs out of the way. We were very relieved to be home. It felt good for many reasons.

Mrs. Angie did not disappoint. She had promised to bring Devon her spaghetti and brownies, when he got home from the hospital. As the week went on we realized Devon's short term memory problems in the hospital were all connected to food. Maybe her spaghetti and brownies would bring back some good memories for him.

The day he insisted he had eaten pizza and cinnamon sticks, Jason and I had eaten that while he was in and out of coherence. He must have remembered that somewhere in his subconscious. The brain is an incredible organ.

The night he insisted he had cheese balls and a piece of his dad's toast was a similar story. The weekend before the surgery, we ordered food from Lincoln Inn, a local restaurant. Jason shared his cheese balls. He also gave Devon a piece of Texas toast, because Dev loves bread.

It was all making sense. But the only thing that mattered to Dev, at that moment, was his spaghetti and brownies. He went after those like a rabid dog. We were all glad that Angie had brought them, as promised.

May 2, 2020, was the dawning of a new day. We started the day with the promise to live life to its fullest and be thankful for every blessing. Devon went straight to work trying to regain his strength and get back into kicking shape.

We went for a family walk around the football field per doctor's orders. Dev was supposed to walk 30 minutes every day. We started day one. He was determined to get back to where he was before the surgery and life-threatening emergency.

I took a picture of him on the field and sent it to his kicking coach. When Devon was in the hospital, Coach Brader had texted him. He expected him to be on the field in a week or two. So there we were, on the field.

The following day, Bryce could not wait any longer. He just had to come see his best friend. With COVID in the air, we were cautious. We knew Devon needed Bryce as much as Bryce needed Devon. They did some social distancing downstairs playing XBox. I told them to keep the jokes to a minimum. The last thing we needed was a staple to pop out. This was a difficult challenge because there was always lots of laughter when those two were together.

We were approaching one week since all hell had broken loose. I was really struggling with the "what ifs." I would lie awake and think about how things could have turned out differently. That feeling I had the night before his surgery was haunting me.

I tried to tell myself I was overreacting because there was only a three percent chance of things going wrong. I was struggling with the fact that the three percent chance had happened. At the same time, I was also feeling very blessed that we were home. He was laughing and playing video games with a friend. I was very anxious about his upcoming follow-up appointment. I did not want to go back to KU Medical Center.

53

Confirmation

THE FOLLOWING TUESDAY, MAY 5, as I parked at KU Medical Center, I found myself emotional again. Walking through those doors was not going to be easy. Everything came rushing back to me. I was sad, angry, but more importantly very thankful. I did not want to be there. I never wanted Devon to be there again either, but it was necessary.

We met with his life-saving heart surgeon. He was amazed at how well Devon was doing. The doctor even surprised Dev by going ahead and removing his staples from his chest incision. He told him it would be another 7- 8 weeks for a full recovery. He talked about the new device and about possibly implanting it in 2-3 weeks, which seemed soon.

The heart surgeon went on to tell us more details about the day of Devon's medical emergency during heart surgery. We were filled in on all the things that went wrong. He bragged on how everyone in that operating room pulled together to save Devon's life. The doctor did confirm he had coded for 13 minutes. He was doing everything he could to ensure Devon would come back to us. The heart surgeon admitted to not knowing what capacity Dev would live. In that moment in the OR, he did everything possible to keep him alive.

He apologized for the wire still being in Devon's body. When the other surgeon had suggested they go ahead and open Devon's heart and get the wire out, he refused. His goal was to repair the tear, stop the bleeding, and keep oxygen going to the brain. The heart surgeon knew he had needed to close him up as soon as possible. His professional opinion was that Devon's body could not endure any more trauma. They did what they could to stabilize him as soon as possible.

The heart surgeon was pleased to hear how well Devon was doing. He confessed that Devon had really scared him. These words sent chills up my spine. It was another true testament to Devon's strength and determination. The doctor's words were also a testimony that he was not done on this Earth. He had a purpose. Devon was a true miracle.

The next step was talking to the original ICD surgeon about Devon's subcutaneous implantation. We could use him and do the next surgery sooner. The other choice was to stick with Dr. T., and do it later in the summer, possibly the end of June.

It was a big decision. Dev was really tired of the life vest, but we were not sure we could take him back to KU. Going back to the surgery center to have a procedure, after all we had endured, was an overwhelming thought. While I know this procedure wasn't supposed to be difficult, we had heard that before.

54

Nurses Day

MAY SIXTH IS NATIONAL NURSES DAY. The one in 2020 hit me hard. I was very thankful for all of Devon's nurses. They were very good to him. All of them were truly pulling for him.

We experienced nurses from one personality extreme to the other. But the one constant was they did a great job. These people genuinely cared about Devon. Each of them was most concerned about his well-being. In the beginning, we experienced the normal side of their job. As our process progressed, it transitioned into them actually being scared for their patient.

At one point I was a little upset because I could read their eyes. They were full of sorrow and sympathy. I asked Jason, "Why do they look at us like that?"

As Devon continued to get better, he surprised them. The sorrow and sympathy turned into hope and admiration. It was then that I realized they genuinely cared about Devon. They worried about him and celebrated his victories.

Once things started to go in the right direction, I had a conversation with two of the nurses. I asked them to be honest. I told them I could see how scared they were. I asked if they were surprised Devon was doing so well. They were both brutally honest. They didn't expect him to be doing well at all.

They both told me that they left their shift that night and called to put him on their prayer chains at church. They admitted to having a very hard time hiding their fears from us. They prayed very hard.

One of them informed me she had lost an older patient a week before Devon's surgery. She just could not bear to lose another one, especially one so young. She called her mom that night. She couldn't give any details but cried with her and asked her to pray for Devon.

The other said he was a miracle. They didn't see those types of miracles very often! Multiple nurses and doctors who were no longer on his case came by to see him to check with their own eyes how well he was doing.

On this very special Nurses Day, I could not help but reflect on these conversations. The fact that they were very selfless in their acts of kindness. Nursing is a very hard job. They definitely deserve a day for recognition and to be celebrated.

I knew what the nurses said about Devon being a miracle was true. Not long after the situation, it became a fact in my mind. It is interesting how God works. We never know how or when, but he will show up in a mighty way.

Later in the year, I took my dog to the local dog groomer, and she asked about Devon. She told me she had prayed hard for him. She had put him on her church prayer chain. I thought it was sweet of her. I had misunderstood and thought she was talking about her church in

Lincoln. She was talking about her hometown church which was near Kansas City.

She had a friend who reached out to all current and past church members to pray for a kid that her daughter was trying to help as a nurse. She said the details were vague. After she heard about Devon, she knew the prayers were for him. The dates, timelines, and severity of it lined up.

I had a huge smile, knowing the nurse really did call her mother. She had begged her to pray for Devon with her. She was really that invested in his well-being.

It gave me chills to know that this had come full circle. If anyone doubted the miracle that had taken place in our lives, they could not doubt it anymore. This was definitely proof that we had witnessed and received a miracle from God.

55

Counting Blessings

AS THE WEEKS WENT ON WE HAD MORE and more to be thankful for. Our friends and family really stepped up big to help us. We were very appreciative and blessed by them.

One thing in particular was the meal train. Angie had graciously set this up for us. Angie knows I am not good at accepting help. She did not ask for permission, she just said, "Sorry but I did this." I did not know it at the time, but it was needed and appreciated very much.

Devon had some social distance porch visits and enjoyed some great food. Angie made sure to get Devon that "pizza and cinnamon sticks" he thought he had already eaten.

Levi and Gabe came by and brought food. Of course, Marsha brought her famous mac and cheese. If you have not been blessed by this, you are missing out.

Callie Jo and Carsyn, friends of Devon's from school, came with a huge box of Devon's favorite snacks. They brought prayer notes from other people, and pictures. It was neat to see everyone step up for our family, but the biggest blessing was seeing all of these students stepping up for our kid!

On May 21, 2020, we were finally able to see Dr. T. She was happy. I had been keeping her updated the entire time. The last time she had physically seen Devon, he was still unconscious.

Her first words to him were, "Hey there Devon, welcome back, you scared us!" While Devon seemed to be doing great, she said that she would feel more comfortable waiting four more weeks to implant the device.

She explained that his body had gone through too much trauma and she did not want to put him under anesthesia so soon. He needed additional time to heal before another surgery. This seemed like a wise choice to Jason and me.

Dr. T. was still concerned about Devon's brain function. He seemed fine, but she wanted to do a brain scan to make sure. They needed to check for any underlying permanent damage.

The medical team did an echo to check his heart and it was great. It showed no permanent heart damage. Dr. T's nurse would call us the next week with a date for surgery. The next surgery recovery would only be two weeks if all went well.

The ICD replacement surgery was scheduled for June 22. Devon was chomping at the bit to get to do things. He was ready to get back to kicking, basketball, golf, and running. He was also excited for things he hadn't done for more than seven years like bench press, pushups, and pullups.

56

The Replacement

DEVON'S BEAT WAS SCHEDULED and going to happen. After all that we had been through, this one was especially important to us. We knew that this was part of our goal and mission.

Devon's Beat happened on June 12 and 13, 2020. Even though he had his life vest on, Devon walked and jogged the 5K. It was absolutely beautiful to witness. Devon was bound and determined that he was going to walk and jog the entire 5K. His life vest may have gone off a time or two, but no ambulances were called.

His best friend Bryce walked with him. Bryce had been Devon's support through this entire process. He was able to give him comfort that no one else could provide. The two of them shared a really special bond.

Drew and Carter came from St. Louis again. This year, Drew had decided winning was not important. He had already proved he could win in the past. He wanted to cross the finish line with Devon. It was a cool moment for them as well.

We were able to raise over $15,000 to go toward helping kids and their families. Once again Lincoln and the surrounding area showed up. This money would help give kids screening that could potentially save their lives. It was a great day.

June 22, 2020 finally came. Time for the ICD replacement surgery. We were glad we went with Dr. T. and Children's Mercy for this surgery. We trusted her.

When I walked in there, it didn't bring back those horrible feelings. She had literally pumped Devon's heart with her hands, willing him back to life. Another comfort was that Dr. T. required an emergency surgeon in the OR with her as per Children's Mercy policy.

She apologized a few times for what happened at KU. Dr. T. really wished she would have waited and done it herself. Not because the vein would not have torn with her, the extraction might have been safer with the heart surgeon present in the room the whole time of the procedure. This is the protocol in children's hospitals.

It was a four-hour procedure. Everyone at the hospital assured us he was in good hands. I was very uneasy, but nothing like Dev's previous replacement surgery. I truly believed she was going to take care of my kid. Dr. T. was going to place the subcutaneous ICD on Devon's left side right under his armpit. They kept us posted the whole time, and the surgery went great.

The recovery nurse said Dev was the sweetest young man. When we got in there, he was all smiles and thumbs up. He was very tired though. He was in and out, sleeping most of the afternoon.

I could see he had a big weight lifted off his shoulders. To be honest, we all had a big weight lifted off of us. After all we had been through, it seemed like things were going in a very positive direction. We were all anxious to get back to our "normal" lives.

When Devon got released the rest was history. He was off to

bigger and better things. That drive to be successful in everything he did was stronger than ever. Funny how a near-death experience can do that to a person.

57

On To Thayer

DEVON WAS FULLY CLEARED July 21, 2020. Not just cleared to return back to the things he was doing before—cleared to do more. It was good to get more than we expected for once. He did not waste any time. Immediately he started doing push ups, pull ups, and bench press. It seemed like the longest 3 months of his life, but he was very thankful.

Johnie Logue did another newspaper article on Devon and his miraculous recovery. It was just in time for the Thayer heart screenings. I had been waiting for this day for a very long time.

The July 25 heart screenings in Thayer finally arrived. We were going to be able to screen Thayer kids in memory of Coach Bryan Tate, as planned. We waited until his family and the town was ready, but we were still blessed to bring heart screenings there in memory of Coach Tate.

When the day finally came, I was able to meet some of his beautiful family. His wife Angela Tate was very sweet, and very helpful with spreading the word about the screenings. She made sure to get the word out to "their" football boys. They also donated $1,500 toward the cost of heart screenings. She was extremely involved. I was thankful she shared her story about Bryan.

Without that story, I would not have known to reach out to Thayer. We also met Brandon and Arthur Tate, Bryan's brothers. Brandon was playing football at Quincy University. The family had been headed to watch him play when they lost Bryan. Brandon was grateful to not only bring screenings to Thayer in memory of his brother, but he was relieved to be tested. Many heart conditions are genetic and that was a concern for the entire Tate family.

Thank God, Brandon and Arthur were fine. Brandon was very cordial, and made sure to talk to Devon. In their conversation he talked about Quincy University and how much he loved it. He mentioned Arthur was going there too.

Brandon told Devon that they were losing their punter and kicker after next year, he should look them up. With COVID they weren't going to have a normal season, but he mentioned coming to see them in the spring. None of our family had actually even heard of Quincy University until then. I started researching it. We were hoping they'd have a camp soon.

We screened 63 kids that day. Of those screened, three had to be referred to a cardiologist. One was the daughter of the administrator who helped me schedule the screenings in Thayer. They were extremely appreciative.

I had been saying since 2012, "Everything happens for a reason." Well after this horrific summer, things were starting to look up and make sense. Next up for the Devon's Beat foundation, heart screenings in Windsor, Missouri.

58

The Virus

IN EARLY AUGUST, JASON WASN'T FEELING WELL and knew he couldn't go to work. Due to COVID, everyone was on edge. Later that morning he had a fever. For work, he had to be tested when a fever was present. Off he went to the clinic. The test was positive. This required the rest of us to be quarantined with him for 10 days.

I had sinus infection symptoms, but both boys seemed fine. The health department wanted the three of us to test as well. Devon and I both turned up positive but not Dawson. This was extremely odd to me. It didn't matter what I thought, we were all quarantined.

Jason was truly sick. I was getting concerned about him. The rest of us were fine. For now, we were all stuck with each other at the house. This virus was no fun.

Because of our COVID quarantine, Devon was missing the first 10 days of football practice. In the state of Missouri, high school football players are required to have 14 practices before they can play a game. He would not have his mandatory 14 practices, because of our quarantine. That meant he would not be able to play in the first game, at the very least. It was his senior year, and he was missing his first home game. We were sad for him. I honestly went to a bitter place, only focusing on the negatives in our lives. I was being childish and very negative. I was crying about Dev having to go through something again. He had endured so much in his short life.

On August 15, 2020, while going through old pictures of the boys, it hit me. It had been exactly five years since Devon went into cardiac arrest for the second time and was saved by his device.

I cried again thinking, "Seriously, Angela! get a hold of yourself, you are blessed! Maybe you have five or more days left in quarantine, but you have your kids and your health." Jason was doing better too. I made myself stop the "poor me" routine and count my blessings.

59

Happy Birthday!

THE LONG QT SYNDROME DIAGNOSIS not only saved Devon's life, it led to the start of Devon's Beat heart screenings. The screenings directly helped save the lives of others. We needed to remember that every time we were down.

While it was easy to get caught up in the dismal summer we had experienced, I chose to be strong. I realized once again, for the one hundredth-plus time, everything happens for a reason! God is Good! I also remembered the promise I had made to God that I would be happy with whatever blessing we received.

I just had to remember that during bad times, I still had hope. My blessings included a larger-than-life younger son who had to go through the trauma too. Jason was a strong husband and dad who helped us stay above water! Last but not least we have Devon, the walking, talking miracle.

August 28, 2020, Devon turned eighteen! I was blown away at how time had flown by, but often felt like it stood still. It was hard to believe.

I had raised an adult, a smart, mature, athletic adult, that had a heart of gold. Devon had endured more in 18 years than most people do in a lifetime.

That particular day was a Friday. This was the home game Devon had to miss because of not getting in enough practices due to COVID! Oh well. He was alive.

I won't lie, it was hard to see him on the sidelines. I was trying not to dwell on it. I was truly happy to have him with us. He was handling it well, all things considered. I know he was worried about missing games. His mission was to finish high school ball and get recruited to play college ball.

He was looking forward to his birthday party the next day. We were also going to the Windsor heart screenings! It was going to be a great day.

Windsor had a huge turnout. Jessica Heany, who was a friend from a rival youth football team, raised money to help pay for all of the screenings. Everything went great. After spending a few hours with them, Dev and I headed home for a big party night.

This was not necessarily like most teenage parties, but a fun night anyway. Devon was a rare breed. He was always a cautious kid growing up, not ever prone to get wild and crazy.

When he was diagnosed with LQTS, one of the things that could be fatal for him was drinking alcohol. While I hated he had to have this awful condition, I was glad he knew alcohol was bad for him. To date he had not been willing to take that risk.

Devon was the kid who always looked at situations and asked, " Is this safe?" If the answer was no, he would use a different path. This was one of the many things I admired about him.

When he was about seven and Daws was two, we went to the beach for the first time. While we all stood looking at the waves rolling in, I looked over at Devon. I could see concern in his eyes. He wasn't sure why anyone would want to get in water that would knock you over. He did not like going underwater.

Meanwhile, Dawson at age two was running as fast as he could to get to the water. By the time we realized it, we were sprinting to make sure he didn't dive in. He could not swim.

Another time, Devon was mad at me for telling him he couldn't jump off of the boat and go underwater. I apologized and said, "I know it sucks, but I'm not willing to let you take that risk." That was something he was no longer allowed to do with his diagnosis. I told him when he was an adult he would be able to make the decisions on his own.

I asked him, "What is going to be the first thing you do when I can't tell you no anymore?" He thought long and hard and said, "Hmm I don't know. Maybe I will go underwater." He did not care anything about drinking caffeine, because now there are tons of decaf options. It definitely was not going to be drinking alcohol, because to him it did not seem worth it. As soon as that came out of his mouth, Dawson said, "Wait, What!? Never? Not even going to try?" I suggested Dawson shut up, or he'd be grounded until he went to college.

But that was Devon, cautious. I didn't have to worry about him having "real" parties. Now Daws? We will see what happens with that boy. There is no telling what he will get into.

60

Rivals On The Field

A FEW DAYS AFTER THE WINDSOR HEART screenings, we got news that a life threatening condition had been found. There were also four others with non-life threatening heart conditions that needed to be checked by a cardiologist. This was the reason we were doing this!

The life threatening condition was Wolff-Parkinson-White (WPW) syndrome It is a heart condition present at birth. That means it's a congenital heart defect. People with WPW syndrome have an extra pathway for signals to travel between the heart's upper and lower chambers. This causes a fast heartbeat. Changes in the heartbeat can make it harder for the heart to work as it should.

The kid was 12-year old Chase Hampton. He had competed against Dawson in youth sports for several years. Chase was a very active kid. Thank goodness his condition was treatable.

He had to have a procedure. Before they knew the severity of it, they had to pull him from football practice. He was scared. His family was scared. It brought back a flood of emotions.

How do you tell a family in fear you are glad you found this condition? Luckily, I didn't have to. They told me. We quickly joined forces and decided his story should be told.

We needed to reach more kids in surrounding areas. That's what we did. We joined forces and did a KY3 interview introducing Chase and his family. We promoted our upcoming "Rivals on the Field" heart screenings in Lincoln. The "Rivals" heart screening was going to be on October 17 and 18, 2020.

Windsor and other local schools were pretty shaken up to know that a seemingly very active kid had this underlying condition. Everyone in that area was paying attention. They wanted to get their kids signed up. Word was spreading fast. "Rivals on the Field" heart screening was going to be big.

My friend Jessica and Chase's mom, Presley, were helping get the word out. They were spreading more awareness and getting very generous donations. This prompted a few other rival schools to participate. Tipton and Cole Camp started soliciting donations too.

61

Friday Night Football

DEVON WAS BACK ON THE FOOTBALL FIELD on Friday nights. We were thrilled to see it. His senior season had that small setback because of COVID. We could see it was starting to gain momentum.

This year was extra exciting because he was fully released. Not to just kick and punt, but with his new device and a special padded shirt, he was allowed to play other positions. He was released to play defense and possibly a little offense at times.

This was exciting and a bit terrifying. Dev told me he was fine, and he knew how to handle it. I trusted him. All of these years he had proven himself by handling every situation in the best way possible.

Every year since his diagnosis, he had played basketball and knew how to do it safely. So here we were with a kicker, punter, defensive back, and wide receiver. The town of Lincoln was caught off guard the first time they saw number four line up as a wide receiver. I had lots of questions from people. Many had some major concerns. By this point, my response was, "He says he's got this and I have to trust him."

In his second game of the season, Devon lined up as a wide out on a PAT. I was nervous, wondering if the ball would go to him. Sure enough, the play was called to Dev! He caught it for his first non-kicking points in his high school career.

I was screaming and crying like a maniac. The crowd went wild. There were many tears in those stands that night. It was very comforting to know how much our town loved and supported Devon. This small town was one of the reasons we made it through so many hard times. They always had our backs. There they were, kids, moms, and even some dads with tears in their eyes.

Local newspaper sports reporter, Johnie Logue, wrote something interesting in the paper after that night. It said, "Tipton had no idea why that PAT meant so much to Lincoln. They were losing by 30 points. To Devon, his family, and his friends it meant *the world*."

He was told he could never play football again, so he kicked instead. They had told us the previous spring he might not wake up from a coma. Even if he did, they didn't know if he would be the same. Guess what, he wasn't the same. Devon was better. Who would have thought we would be in this place, at this time. Ole Daws was right once again. Devon needed his cleats and not just for kicking this time. It was a night we will never forget!

62

Trust Me

DEVON DECIDED TO GO to a football camp at Quincy University, in Quincy, Illinois. It was a three and a half hour drive from Lincoln. He was willing to do whatever he needed to do to get a look from college coaches. We had actually not heard of this school until we met Brandon Tate in Thayer at the screenings.

Brandon told Devon to come on up and join them for the camp. It was such a neat campus, and the coaches were great. This particular camp didn't have many kickers or punters. Wait, it had none. They expected more at the next camp. We couldn't make that one, so Coach Borghardt, the offensive coordinator, told him to come anyway.

Next thing we knew, Devon was on the field before anything started. It was just him, Coach Borghardt, and Brandon Tate, who was the long snapper. Oh my goodness, he was on display for the world. Well, not the whole world, but at least the other campers and families to see. He was as cool as a cucumber once again and punted really well.

After camp, he also kicked. Coach Borghardt came to meet us after it was over and bragged about Devon. Coach said he was a really strong punter and wanted to keep in touch. He got our numbers and we went on a tour of the facilities and campus.

It was exciting and overwhelming. On the way home, Dev talked about how comfortable he was punting. He brought up a conversation we had a couple of weeks prior. Dev told us, although he loved to kick, he really thought he should focus more on punting. It felt more natural. He felt better about it. It might be his path to college.

His desire to focus on punting caught me by surprise. I was very confused! I even called Coach Brader, his kicking coach from St. Louis, and tattled on Devon. Coach Brader said he would talk to him. His instructions to Devon were to continue doing both. Devon agreed he wasn't going to stop kicking. He just wanted to focus on being recruited as a punter.

I am not positive, but I think I got a huge "I told you so, Mom!" on the way home from Quincy that day. Another "trust me Mom," moment in the books.

63

The Payoff

ON OCTOBER 17 AND 18, the "Rivals on the Field" heart screening was a huge success. We screened 109 kids. Ten kids were identified to have risk factors. Chase and his mom were there helping share his story.

Later on in the football season, Devon had another great moment. Lincoln was winning the game and was stopped on a third down on the other team's side of the field inside Dev's field goal range. The coaches decided to kick a field goal to preserve the lead. They lined up for the kick and it was a fake. Devon rolled out with the ball and threw a touchdown pass. It was his first TD pass since fourth grade.

Believe it or not I went crazy again, cheering and crying. The stands erupted with yelling and screaming. We went on to win that game! It was a great night!

Devon went on another college visit. This time to Missouri S&T, located in Rolla, Missouri. Rolla was a little closer to Lincoln than Quincy, only two hours away. S&T was a very nice school and well known for its academics. I could tell Devon didn't love it as much as he loved Quincy.

November 11, 2020, Devon received a phone call from Coach Borghardt with his very first college football offer. Coach was anxious to get Devon back to campus to show him why he should choose Quincy as his school.

In early December we went on the "official" visit. I could just tell Devon loved it. Quincy University had a great atmosphere on the college campus. The coaches created a family bond with their players in the football program. All of the people in the town seemed to rally around the University.

I wanted to hate it. It was three and half hours from home. My mama heart was not sure I could take that distance. I could tell Dev loved it. Honestly, I could not pretend to hate it. I loved it too.

On the way home, I told Devon, "This is it, isn't it?" Dev didn't even want to see if he received other offers. In his heart he knew where he belonged. He had found his new home.

On December 7, 2020, Devon Lee Parrott committed to Quincy University in Illinois. He was going to be their next punter. It was fantastic to see all of his hard work pay off.

A few days later we received news that Devon's kicking friend, Drew Lenzen, from St. Louis, had also committed to Quincy. He was going to be their next kicker. He and Dev were going to get to play together. As a family we felt all of the emotions. We were extremely excited! We were happy. We were proud. We were amazed. Most of all, we were thankful.

What are the odds? Well, I can tell you what the odds are. Only 7.5 percent of high school football players go on to play at the collegiate level. Much less a player from a small high school of only one hundred and twenty students. My kid, who had been close to death several times, made it happen.

To top it off, Devon had scored a 29 on his ACT. That was definitely something to celebrate as well. There is no doubt we were feeling thankful and blessed.

December was pretty busy. Basketball was starting to get rolling. There was also excitement in the community with the news of Devon's commitment to Quincy.

Dev was named Benton County Enterprise (our local county newspaper) athlete of the year. In addition, he received all conference, all district, and academic all-state kicker.

One day I got tagged in a post on facebook. It was from the mom of a local youth football player. The boy had gotten a football for Christmas. He immediately went outside and started punting like Devon. Dev was someone's hero. Someone other than me!

64

The Dotted Line

LOOKING BACK ON 2020, I did not take for granted that all of my prayers had been answered. Devon was alive. He not only woke up, but he knew who he was. He was able to get his memory back. To top it off he was still athletic and a very smart student.

National Signing Day was February 3. That day was very exciting. He got a phone call the night before on what to do. The table was set up in the high school gym. Dev signed his letter of intent to punt for the Quincy University Hawks.

That was a fun, inspiring day that he got to share with his friends, family, teachers, and coaches. He not only received a football scholarship, he was awarded a nice academic scholarship as well.

We were gearing up to host a heart screening in Ozark, Missouri, at the travel baseball team facility where Dawson played. The director of Marucci Baseball was excited to host the event. They helped raise money by holding an indoor home run derby. The big heart screening event in Ozark was set for March 6 and 7, 2021. This was going to help us screen even more kids.

Basketball season was going well. Devon was playing some of the best basketball of his life. He had a girlfriend now. We loved her from the beginning. Jenna Vandaveer shared his love for basketball. The sport helped create a bond between them. He was clearly very smitten with her.

We had the date set for our Ninth Annual Devon's Beat 5K. It was going to be April 23 and 24, 2021. We were looking forward to raising some useful funds to help with heart screenings.

As a family, we were counting our blessings and enjoying the basketball season. Devon's team had their ups and downs. At the end of the season, they were able to go on a pretty great run. The Lincoln boys ended up winning districts for the first time in 15 years. I guess when I told him, "Don't suck!" He took it seriously.

Devon had gone from being told he could never play the sport he loved again to being one of the vital players of his championship team. He worked hard and played harder. He loved every moment of it. Jason and I just soaked up every minute of getting to watch him compete.

It was nice to see him excel in something he loved. He received all-conference, all- district and academic all-state awards in basketball. The team came up a little short in the sectional game. Dev was sad for it to be over. But now it was on to golf.

65

More Blessings

THINGS WERE STARTING TO COME AROUND for the screenings in Ozark at Midwest Marucci. Between some parents from Dawson's travel baseball team, Zone One, and Marucci, we had $5,000 donated already.

I received a text from a mom of one of the teammates on Dawson's team. It was Beau's mom. Beau had joined the team a year earlier. I am an outgoing girl and was quick to chat up his mom, Kerry. They seemed like a great family. Daws was getting closer with Beau every tournament. It didn't take long for Kerry and me to hit it off.

I received a text one day from Kerry that said she had some donation money for me. I was super excited. She said she had been working on it for a while. She had it finalized and had a check for Devon's Beat for $20,000! What?!

I could not believe what I was reading and questioned her. She explained to me that her family had a foundation called the Fuldner

Family Foundation. They had decided to make Devon's Beat one of their charities to support in 2021!

While reading, I had tears streaming down my face. I could not even believe it. In eight years of hard work, one Devon's Beat fundraiser had never raised $20,000 in a weekend, let alone a single donation.

I am not complaining about the amount of money we raised before the donation. It was amazing. I just could not believe I got more in one check than any single Devon's Beat had raised. I told her how special it was to me and our foundation. When I told Devon and the rest of the family about it they were blown away.

On the sixth of March we got off to a great start. All of Dawson's team-mates were getting screened, as well as many other Marucci players. Angela Tate, from Thayer, even came by to see how it was going and to support us.

Unfortunately, Kerry was out of town for one of her other kids' sports. I was able to meet Beau's grandma, who brought him to the screening. Her name was Ginny, she was Kerry's mom. I was very happy to meet her.

I knew she really didn't want a big deal to be made about the family and their donation. I asked Ginny's permission to introduce her to Eric and David. She was excited to meet them and learn more about their operation. She seemed like an intriguing woman. I was glad to meet her and to thank her for the generous family donation.

While they wanted to stay anonymous, I wanted to shout it from the rooftop. I still just couldn't believe their generosity. She waited patiently for Beau to get tested. Then she was on her way. We sent them off with hugs and thank yous from our family.

A few moments later a mom who was having her kid tested came up to me. She said, "Excuse me, but the lady that just left, was that Ginny Fuldner?" I nervously said, "Yes," because I thought maybe she overheard us talking. I was trying to keep them anonymous. She asked if she had already left. I said, "Yes, why?" She responded, "Oh darn I haven't seen her in years, she is such a great lady and such an inspiration."

I must have looked confused. She said, "Do you not know who she is?" I quietly said, "A grandma to one of my son's friends." She said, "Oh girl, she's an Olympic gold medalist! She won gold in the 1964 Olympics as a swimmer." What? Why did I not know this? The lady went on to say, she was one of the kindest, most humble people she had ever met.

When she left, I went to Google. Sure enough she won gold in the 400 meter freestyle and bronze in the 100 meter backstroke in Tokyo at the 1964 Olympics.

I texted Kerry ASAP. I said, " Um, I did not know your mom is an Olympic gold medalist!" She said, "Well I guess not. I am sorry." I explained to her how I had found out. She went on to tell me how proud she was of her moms story. Her mom was very humble and did not speak of herself much. For this reason, neither did her family. I got it and completely understood. It is not like you can introduce yourself and say, "I am Kerry and my mom won a gold medal." More and more I began to love and admire this family.

The two-day screening event went extremely well! The event, including the Fuldner Family Foundation donation, raised $25,000! It was a great weekend.

One of the promises we gave to the Fuldner family was that we would also go to Monett to have screenings. That was their hometown. I later learned Ginny and her husband Chris donated to the YMCA. The pool was called the Ginny and Chris Fuldner Family Aquatics Center.

The Monett screening was set for December 11, 2021. We also scheduled a screening in Boonville, Missouri for November 20. The calendar was filling up.

Our Ninth Annual Devon's Beat raised around $20,000! Between Devon's Beat, Marucci, and Kerry's family, we were at a record $45,000!

66

The Season of Lasts

DEVON'S SENIOR YEAR was quickly coming to a close. He had a good golf season. I am glad that he learned to enjoy golf. For a while it looked like the only sport he would be able to compete in.

We had lots of "lasts" to end the school year. Devon had his last National Honor Society banquet, last band concert, and last golf match. I was trying to soak in as much as I could. The remainder of the school year went very fast. Time seemed to move quickly in the spring of the school year. Before we knew it, the last day of school had arrived. It was hard to believe that Devon was already graduating. It had been a fantastic year, but it went way too fast. I was not ready for it to be over. I was struggling to keep up with the fast paced end of his schooling.

Graduation was such a blur, however one thing does stand out in my mind. I was on the school board. Lincoln High School allows school board members to be on the stage at graduation. When Devon's name was called to walk across the stage, I was able to hand him his diploma. In my mind, it was the perfect graduation moment. I will cherish it forever!

His graduation party was a huge success. Many people came to wish him well and celebrate with us. Devon was very surprised when his friends Drew and Carter showed up from St. Louis. It was a wonderful night!

The summer before Dev left for Quincy went very quickly. We did have some fun. We tried to spend as much time together as a family as possible, because we knew we could not get that time back. Dawson had baseball tournaments many weekends. Devon did not love them, but he came along anyway. He connected with parents and made some little friends in the form of the player's younger siblings. They adored him.

Devon's senior trip was planned. We decided to go to Myrtle Beach, South Carolina. It just so happened that Kerry's family had a beach house in North Carolina only a half an hour away from Myrtle Beach. We were there at the same time and were able to spend a day with them.

Devon, Jason, Cory, who is Kerry's husband, and Chris, her dad, went and played golf. Ginny, Kerry, the kids, and I went to the beach. It was a perfect day. The weather was beautiful and the warm sand and sun was just what we needed. The icing on the cake was Ginny telling us her story of how she became an Olympic gold medalist. It was very inspirational. I encourage everyone to research it.

Doomsday finally came. On August 8, 2021, it was time to take Dev to Quincy. Three and a half hours seemed like a long way from home. I was very excited for him, but very sad, worried, and scared. This was absolutely going to test my resolve.

There were two things that made it better for me. He had his room-mate, Drew. They had known each other for years, kicking together in St. Louis with David Brader. In addition, his coaches worked very hard to create a family-like atmosphere for the boys.

When we got in the car and pulled away from him, I cried my eyes out. I did notice a tear in Dev's eye too. My heart was ripped out. It is hard to leave them on their own. I could not get a hold of myself. It literally took a full week for me to pull it together. I was truly happy for him. But my heart was broken. Going into his room made it worse. I just went in there and cried.

67

Life Goes On

I MADE EVERY EXCUSE to make trips to Quincy. He redshirted his freshman year. It did not matter, I was still there for most home games. It was great! But every time I left I cried. It was getting a little easier each time, because I was able to see how much he loved it.

We had another family scare in 2021. Dawson passed out one August night while trying to nurse a bloody nose. We didn't think too much about it. Later, in September, he woke up one morning and was about to get in the shower when he passed out again.

I was upstairs and heard a huge bang. I ran downstairs and I found him passed out in the bathroom. I couldn't tell if he had hit his head. It took me a minute to get him up. Once I did, he was immediately sick to his stomach, sweaty, and cold.

I got him dressed and kept him awake as I drove him to the doctor. Although he had been tested three times, his pediatrician decided he needed to be tested again for LQTS. I was very upset and worried.

Jason and I did not think we could do it all again. Mentally I did not know if I could handle it. Instead of waiting on a Children's Mercy appointment, we took him to My HeartCheck in Kansas City. This was ironic, because they got us Dawson's results very quickly and he appeared to be fine.

We took the results to Children's Mercy. The doctor was able to confirm he did not have a heart condition. Instead he suffered from Postural Orthostatic Tachycardia Syndrome (POTS).

POTS is a condition that causes a number of symptoms when you transition from lying down to standing up. Symptoms include a fast heart rate, dizziness, and fatigue. While there's no cure, several treatments and lifestyle changes can help manage the symptoms of POTS.

Dawson's treatment was to drink more water, eat more salt, and not get up too quickly. Luckily we have had no other episodes. Thank God!

Meanwhile, Devon was enjoying college, and Dawson was doing much better. Dev's girlfriend Jenna, now like a member of the family, made her one-thousandth career point in high school basketball. Dev was dating someone who made the 1,000 point club. That is a big deal at Lincoln High School.

We generously received another $20,000 check from the Fuldner Family Foundation. I wanted someone to pinch me. I could not make this up. All these hard years of raising money and only being able to schedule screenings as money came in, I was now ahead of the game. I could schedule future screenings with no financial worries. We could now offer screenings at no charge to anyone who needed it, regardless of their financial situation.

68

Loving Life

2022 WAS PRETTY UNEVENTFUL as far as Devon's health went. We were very busy as usual. Devon went back to Quincy in January. Again, this was very hard for me.

We had set the date for our Tenth Annual Devon's Beat for the end of April. It was hard to believe that it had been 10 years.

Dev made the dean's list for his first college semester with a GPA of 3.91. We were very proud of him. With all of the medical issues that could have affected his cognitive ability, that GPA was amazing.

Devon was getting involved in his community. He did the polar plunge with a group of friends for the Special Olympics. It was a very rewarding experience.

He also attended a prayer group for the people in Ukraine during the war. He did not want to go alone. I told him that he needed to go because these people needed prayer just like he had in previous years. He needed to pay it forward. Devon went and was blessed for doing so.

At the prayer group, he met an older lady who had no family. She was impressed with Devon and his willingness to pray for those in need. She gave him 50 dollars. He tried to refuse it, but she said she had no family and felt led to give it to him.

Spring ball started. The date for his spring game was scheduled for the same Saturday as Devon's Beat. I was not missing either and made it work. Devon's Beat went off without a hitch. This would be the first time Devon would miss the event. On Friday night after practice, he drove up to surprise me at the dance. Jenna knew he was coming and was there waiting for him when he walked in. It was an amazing moment and made my day. He came to breakfast before the 5K Saturday morning, but couldn't run because he had to get back to his spring game. As soon as it was over, I headed to Quincy. I was exhausted, but thankful I could get it all done.

In May Devon was back home, and he accepted a paid internship at Golden Valley Physical Therapy in Clinton. He was interested in pursuing a degree in PT. In addition, Dev worked a couple days for his dad. Once again he had made the dean's list.

Jenna graduated and was accepted to Quincy University. The summer went too fast. Before we knew it Devon and Jenna were headed back to Quincy.

Football started, and although there was a six-year senior ahead of him, Devon was looking forward to the season. He practiced hard and got a chance to punt a few times. The most important time was at homecoming. He had a big fan club. I once again went to all the games regardless of whether he played or not.

In November, we received another precious gift of $20,000 from the Fuldner Family Foundation. I was still in awe of their generosity. I was able to finally release that their family foundation had made their yearly donations. They believed in the cause and supported it wholeheartedly.

69

Still Work To Be Done

DEVON ONCE AGAIN MADE THE DEAN'S LIST for the fall semester. He was three for three and planned to keep it going. I was still impressed with his academic ability.

We set the date for Devon's Beat for April 22, 2023. The donations were coming in. We were very optimistic for another big turn out.

In February, I heard about a Missouri Valley College basketball player named Jace Lance, from Marshall, Missouri. During practice he had collapsed. Thankfully, he was saved by an AED and CPR performed by his dad, the coach. He was diagnosed with a heart condition he knew nothing about and had an ICD implanted. I reached out to his mom, and before we knew it we were talking about hosting heart screenings in Marshall, in honor of Jace.

In March Devon called me to tell me he had pain and a mass around the top of his tailbone. The campus nurses thought it was a cyst. I was worried about him and texted his heart doctor. He ordered an ultrasound.

The next day at 11 a.m. the surgeon called me and said it was definitely a cyst. It needed to be removed or drained and they asked him to come in at 12:45 that afternoon. I was scared. I hopped in the car and headed to Quincy.

I prayed they'd wait until I got there before they did anything. They did not. Jenna went with him and put me on speaker phone. She was scared because he was in extreme pain.

They needed to drain it and cut part of it out to do a biopsy. However, it's not that simple. As you know, Dev can't have certain pain meds, anesthesia or even antibiotics.

Jenna was on top of it. She questioned their every move. At one point, she was concerned enough that the doctor went out and called his heart surgeon to make sure what they were doing was OK. He made it through the procedure fine, however he was in so much pain, I decided to bring him home for a few days to keep a watch over him.

We were thankful to have nurse Angie Koll take care of him while he was home. He ended up with several infections including staph and had to be on antibiotics. He was on the mend, but had we not known about his LQTS it could have been worse.

I receive messages and texts about kids dying suddenly of unknown heart conditions pretty regularly. It hits hard, when the death is close to home. I was told about a kid from Salisbury, Missouri. We had just played them in the sectional basketball game. Salisbury had won the game and was preparing for the state games. A starter for the team had died in his sleep just days before they were to play in the state final four. Another terrible reminder of why our mission with Devon's Beat is to create awareness and get kids screened for any Sudden Arrhythmic Death Syndrome!

70

Positive Vibes

I RECEIVED THE MOST AWESOME SURPRISE! Drew worked for QU TV in Quincy. He did an interview with Devon for the station. The boys sent me a video of the interview.

I was brought to tears. Drew asked Devon, " Who is your role model?" Devon said, "My mom, she has always been there for me and pushes me to be a better person. I look up to her the most." WOW!

Drew asked Dev what drove him to be great. He said, "Again, my mom and dad. They push me to be better both academically and athletically. They helped me to get to the collegiate level to play football." Man this kid really knew how to get me crying.

Devon's answer to the moment that he would love to relive was his junior year of high school playing in the state championship football game at Mizzou. It was a great memory for all of us, especially given the surgical emergency which would happen after that.

The time came for the Tenth Annual Devon's Beat 5K, Dance, and Auction, and it went fantastically! It was a little sad because it was the first year Devon missed the event. He had to stay in Quincy for the spring game. I also had to miss the spring game because of Devon's Beat. While we both understood, we were both a little sad. Both went extremely well.

Dev made the dean's list again, this time with a 4.0. He switched his major from physical therapy to business finance. He no longer wanted to be a physical therapist, but decided he wanted to eventually become a day trader. He also received academic all-Great Lakes Valley Conference accolades in football.

Dev spent some time at home in the summer. He worked with his dad at Boone Quarries. August came too soon and he was back at school and back to football, this time as the starting punter.

Devon turned 21 that August. I surprised him with a few friends at Buffalo Wild Wings in Quincy. Jenna and Drew were a big help in planning his surprise party.

Devon had a very good football season. We had a blast going to his football games that fall. It was incredible to see how far he had come. He was definitely a shining example of perseverance.

We received another donation from the Fuldner Family Foundation in November. We were set for a big year. Devon's Beat was scheduled for May of 2024.

71

Pressing On

WE FINALLY GOT OUR MARSHALL screenings scheduled in honor of Jace Lance. We screened 178 kids overall and we found one with Long QT syndrome. He was 15 and he was devastated. His mom reached out to me. I tried to share our story with her, and recommended he go to Children's Mercy. He has done well since his LQTS was discovered and treated. He was back to playing basketball in no time.

The thought of this family starting their LQTS journey brought up many painful memories. It also incited feelings of thankfulness and joy. We had Devon in our lives. Because of our struggle and starting Devon's Beat, they had their son in their lives.

I immediately texted Devon about it. In his typically simplistic thinking he texted back, "He is so lucky." When the mom told her son about Devon's response, it got the first smile out of him in several days.

I told Devon it was because of him. He had allowed me to share his story and start Devon's Beat. He said, "No mom, It's because of you.

You did this!" He has a heart of gold. He never wants credit. He just wants to help other people avoid the trauma he has had to live through and recover from.

Devon got a summer internship at a local bank in Quincy. He wasn't coming home for the summer of 2024. I was very happy for him. It made me sad to not have him in town though. He was getting to learn many different departments at the bank. Life was moving forward. He was starting to live his grown-up life.

Again, Devon made the dean's list. He was six for six now. In May he was inducted into the Sigma Delta Beta Honor Society for business. In addition, Dev received several academic awards.

We hosted our Twelfth Annual Devon's Beat in May, and Devon and Jenna both came and ran in the 5K. It was a fabulous couple of days and we were thankful for the continued support of our community. We were able to raise over $19,000 to go toward future heart screenings.

Quincy Football had a coaching change. Devon was faced with a tough decision. He had some opportunities at the bank in the fall. He was not going to be able to play football and work at the bank. He made the tough decision to improve his career at the bank and walk away from football. It turned out to be an excellent decision. Dev was able to continue to learn and set himself up for a great job after graduation. He has always been wise beyond his years.

At his annual heart doctor appointment we learned of a couple of incidents Devon's ICD had detected, but nothing too serious. We also learned that unless it is an emergency they will probably never remove his old ICD wire from his chest. If they do, it will have to be done at the Mayo Clinic. The procedure is not an easy task, and very few surgeons will even attempt it.

Devon was set to graduate from Quincy University in December

2024, with honors. I was very proud of this kid. He has been the model of resilience and hard work since he was born.

We find ourselves being grateful and thankful. We have been very blessed to get to live the life we have. Our family is keenly aware of the fact that our lives could be vastly different. God saw fit to spare Devon Lee Parrott's life not once, not twice, but three times.

There is no doubt that the Lord had a plan for Devon's life and ours as a family. We will continue to bring awareness to LQTS and other SADS. Our goal is to help as many families as we can.

In November, we once again received the yearly donation from the Fuldner Family Foundation. This year makes $100,000 total they have donated since March of 2021!

Through Devon's Beat fundraising we have generated a total of $178,200 since 2013. This is all from the small town of Lincoln located in Central Missouri. We have simply had an annual 5K with a dance and auction, for the last 12 years and generous donors like the Fuldner Family Foundation.

Devon's Beat and the Fuldner Family Foundation have joined forces to provide screenings in 20 towns in Central Missouri and Northern Arkansas. The funds have paid for the screening of 2,090 kids. We will not quit until we have tested as many as possible.

On December 15, 2024, Devon Lee Parrott had his name called to walk across the stage at Quincy University. Before the ceremony started, I reminded him as only I can, "Don't suck!" He graduated Summa Cum Laude with an overall GPA of 3.9.

Devon, who as a ten-year-old boy, was statistically never supposed to survive a LQTS episode in the hallway of Lincoln Elementary. As a tween he had to be revived in a movie theater by his ICD. As a teenager, he was not supposed to wake up from a coma. Even if he did, Dev certainly was never supposed to have the brain function he previously did. That special guy made it happen. He persevered to that monumental graduation day, and he did it with honors!

To say we were proud is the understatement of the world. We hope to continue the fundraising and screening effort so that others like him can be as successful as he has been. I refuse to let all that we have learned and been through be in vain. We will continue to champion the cause as God allows us too. In May of 2025, DEVON'S BEAT goes on!

Thank you for your purchase of Devon's Beat. Portions of the proceeds of this book go to the Devon's Beat foundation. If you would please consider being a donor to the Devon's Beat foundation, it would be greatly appreciated. Our foundation exists to provide educational awareness and free heart screenings to children around the country and hopefully, eventually the world. If you are interested please scan the QR code below or visit devonsbeat.com.

THANK YOU SO MUCH FOR YOUR SUPPORT!

DEVON'S PERSPECTIVE

THE INITIAL DIAGNOSIS was very emotional for me. I remember being devastated when I first heard that I might not be able to play sports anymore. Looking back on it now, it seems silly that I was so concerned about not being able to compete, but I don't think I fully understood the magnitude of the situation. I did not realize that I was just blessed to be alive. However, for a child who has always loved and played sports, it was very upsetting to hear that I might never play football or basketball ever again.

Getting the first ICD implant caused a mixture of emotions for me. On one hand, I was ready to get it over with, and I was optimistic that this would give me more freedom to do the things that I loved. On the other hand, it seemed like it was all happening very fast, and it was frightening. This was the first surgery I had ever had. I was very nervous.

Learning to kick was a very important part of my journey. It was the first opportunity for me to compete again. I was excited to learn and I enjoyed the whole process. David Brader was my coach. He taught me so much, and was very good to me and my family. Kicking not only allowed me to compete again, but also introduced me to so many new people.

It gave me many new friends, some of which I have stayed friends with for a long time.

Basketball was always my favorite sport growing up, and finally being able to play after such a long hiatus was very exciting. I don't remember much about my first season back since it was such a long time ago. I just remember being so grateful to be on the court again. To get my doctor to approve of me playing basketball, I had to wear a padded shirt under my jersey to protect the ICD. I also had to wear a heart monitor at all times. These things used to annoy me so much.

I remember being very self conscious about them. The padded shirt was very bulky and uncomfortable. The monitor came with a watch that I had to wear at all times. The watch was also bulky and I had to wear a wristband over it. I think the reason I was very self conscious is because I felt like these things were very noticeable. I thought that once people started to notice them, they would look at me differently.

When I first started wearing these items I was in late elementary school and going into junior high. This is the time in a kid's life when they start to care what people think about them and I think that really hit me hard. I didn't know what other people would think about me if they saw me wearing the shirt and the watch. I did not want them to look at me differently.

I vaguely remember my appendix operation and the sicknesses that followed. I mainly remember being in quite a bit of pain after the initial surgery. I could not stand up straight. It just felt like there was a huge gap in my stomach that was missing and it felt very uncomfortable if I stood up straight. The more significant part of 2015 came after the initial sicknesses when I passed out in the movie theater. That was a very strange experience because I wasn't entirely sure what happened. I remember being in the car on the way to the hospital and finally putting together what had just happened. It was pretty scary at first because nothing like that had happened since the initial experience. I don't really remember much else from those events.

My high school football and basketball career before 2020 were pretty normal. I was starting kicker on the football team every year and became the starting punter my junior year. I had fun playing football and it was especially exciting to make it to the state championship two years in a row. Basketball was pretty similar. I didn't get much playing time until my junior year, but basketball was my favorite sport. I always had fun just being on the team.

2020 was a very interesting year to say the least. I was very excited to be getting the new ICD put in because I was told I would have no restrictions. Of course that was very good news. I'm sure mom has elaborated on my inability to recall the events that occurred after my first surgery, but it was an absolute disaster. I remember before the surgery when mom called and told me that I had to go to the hospital immediately. I was extremely worried because she told me that the leads had gone bad (I don't remember exactly what happened). I wasn't sure what that meant. I originally thought that I was going to be electrocuted or something like that. I thought that it was like an exposed wire or something. Even though I was incredibly worried, I was also kind of excited because I would be getting the new ICD put in.

I remember practically nothing from after the surgery. The things that I do remember I have been told are incorrect. I do remember some of the recovery however which was abysmal. For a long time I didn't realize the extent of my injuries. I would try and do things that I was definitely not supposed to do. The soreness and the pain set in pretty quickly afterward. I remember the only exercise I could do for a while was just walking, and I was incredibly slow at that. I always felt lucky that all this had happened over COVID because I didn't miss much of anything since everyone was locked up in their homes.

Getting the new ICD put in was very exciting. It felt like a huge relief because with the old ICD there were many things that I was not allowed to do. Now I had no restrictions. It just felt refreshing.

Senior year football and basketball were very fun. Our football team was pretty mediocre. I think we were just under 500, but of course I had a good time. I was finally allowed to play other positions rather than just kick. I didn't get a ton of playing time, but it was still exciting to play other spots on the field. Basketball season was very exciting. We won the district championship for the first time since 2003. I was the only senior on the team. Senior night was pretty short, but I still got to play with several good friends and had a great time.

Playing football in college was really a dream come true. So many kids dream of playing sports in college and of course I had the same dream. When I started kicking I realized that I really had a chance of playing at the next level. I had such a good time playing in college, and I got a degree to go along with it. I am just very grateful to have had the opportunity.

Hosting Devon's Beat and the heart screenings have been such a big part of my life. My mom has done such a great job organizing everything and bringing it to fruition. None of it would be possible without her. I am just really glad that we have been able to help so many kids get free heart screenings and have raised more awareness around conditions like mine. It really makes me happy when I look back at where this all started and think about everything we have accomplished.

PERSPECTIVES FROM FAMILY AND FRIENDS

Jason — Devon's dad

I'll never forget the day that Ang called me and told me that Devon had fainted in school. From that point on it was a rollercoaster of ups and downs. We went from not being able to enjoy watching him play sports, to finding out he could resume some normal physical activities. Through his first surgery, to the most recent scare, this has been some of the most sad, happy, gut wrenching, tearful, and grateful days of my life. Through everything, we've had the great fortune of having tremendous support from family and friends. With the Devon's Beat fundraiser, Ang has been able to spread awareness and undoubtedly save lives. In reflection over the years since that first phone call, I realized just how strong and special Devon is. He will definitely be able to endure and thrive with all that life has thrown at him.

Debbie — Devon's Grandma

From the time Devon was born, (as with our 3 other grandchildren) we tried to go see him as often as possible; birthdays, school functions, and just to spoil them. As much spoiling as we could get away with anyway.

The first time I learned of anything out of the ordinary with Devon, we were in Little Rock with my son and his family having lunch. My phone rang and when I answered it was Angela telling me Dev had passed out walking down the hall at school. She assured me she was not really worried, but was going to take him to his pediatrician to be on the safe side. My family and I discussed it and we were concerned but not overly so. Devon was a healthy, active in all sports, normal, little boy. Angela called me and said they ran tests and didn't find anything, but to be on the safe side they were sending him to Children's Mercy Hospital to see a heart specialist. Now I was worrying a little, but tried not to show it.

Angela called me on the way to Children's Mercy, but she really didn't think anything was wrong with Devon. When she got the results, I was devastated. We could not believe there was anything wrong concerning his heart. Hearing that he would have to give up sports that he loved made my heart ache for him. I knew how much he loved football and basketball. He was so talented in sports, but if that would keep him alive, then we would find a way to keep him happy and active. I thank God often for giving Devon a chance because we were told that, frequently, the first sign of this condition is death.

I was very moved when Angela put together the first Devon's Beat 5K. Most of the small town of Lincoln showed up to support the cause, and many from surrounding towns. I couldn't stop my tears when I saw so many friends and family come to support Devon and his family. Devon participated and Angela asked me to be there when he finished in case he had issues. I was very scared, but asked God to be with Devon and take care of him. I am thankful that she works to get the word out about this sneaky condition. Maybe it will help bring awareness to Long QT syndrome.

The next scare was when he had to have his ICD implanted. I was scared that he would not respond to the anesthetics and was told they had to stop his heart to make sure it was going to work. That was scary thinking about them stopping his heart. One thing stands out with his little brother. When they let us go back to see Devon before they gave his anesthetic, Dawson just wanted to know why they put a dress on him (referring to the hospital gown).

Another time Angela called and said they were on the way to hospital. This was the movie theater incident. All I could think of this time was we were very blessed he had the ICD to bring him back. God surely has a plan for him.

We were heading to Wisconsin for vacation another time. Devon had to have his appendix removed. Again, we were scared for him to have to undergo surgery. How much more can he take? We luckily found a motel room in Kansas City, there were only a couple rooms available because of so many events going on at the time. We stayed until surgery was over and he was out of recovery.

The biggest scare of all was when they had to replace his ICD. COVID was running rampant and everything was locked down. Angela told us when they took him back and said she would keep us posted. Waiting by the phone, it seemed an eternity until we heard from her. Unfortunately, she didn't have good news. She wasn't sure if he was going to make it or not. This can't be happening. Then she called the next time and said he was going to make it, but might have brain damage. Again, this can't be happening. I had to call other family members to inform them. We all cried together. We packed bags and went to her house to be with Dawson.

Each time I talked with Angela, I had more and more hope. When Devon came home a few days later I could not believe how good he looked. Thank you God again. While I will always be concerned with Devon's health, I no longer worry as much about him

Dawson — Devon's Brother

Being Devon's younger brother, there is a majority of the timeline that I do not remember at all. There are also times that I did not realize everything that was really going on. From hearing my mom tell the story of the process, to remembering some situations, it really blows my mind to know everything he went through. He has endured quite a bit to get where he is today.

Although I may be bigger, faster, stronger, smarter, better looking, and yes mom likes me more, Dev is still pretty cool. OK, let's put all of that aside. As much as we fought in our younger years, got in trouble by mom, and I tried to get him in trouble, it truly is amazing to think of how strong he is. He really is the best big brother anybody could ever ask for.

Teresa — School Nurse

My main memory of the day Devon collapsed in the hall, is his teacher sitting beside him on the cot in my office. As I took his vital signs, checked his blood sugar, and asked question after question she was there. I felt like she was looking at me like, "Aren't you going to do something?" but I knew she didn't know there was a reason for how I was handling him.

As a school nurse, especially in a rural small town like Lincoln, you have to be prepared for anything and you have to remain calm. During my assessment and our conversation, I found out that Devon had experienced something similar while watching cartoons when he was "little" as he put it. This was definitely concerning to me and I wanted his physician to know every little piece of information I could find to help his assessment.

If I remember correctly, there wasn't anything of concern with his vital signs, but kids just don't "pass out" for no reason. When I called

Devon's mom, Angela, I knew I had to present the information as calmly as possible. I did not want her becoming so upset that she would be unable to get Devon to his physician.

God was definitely watching out for all of us that day. Devon got up and acted as if nothing happened to him except to say, "that was weird." His grandparents from out of town just happened to be in town and with his mom when I called. His mom picked him up and took him to his pediatrician, then on to Children's Mercy.

Even though we didn't need it that day, our school already had two AEDs in place. I never really thought too much about the AEDs until this happened with Devon. Ours were kept in a cabinet in the high school office in case we would need them for someone at a game or some other event. By the time I left my position in 2017, our school district had five AEDs. One in the high school gym, one in the elementary hall, one in the football field house and two more for travel purposes. One AED was always designated to go with Devon to all trips and games. The other travel AED went with me to every home and away football game. For a school with an enrollment *of* around 500 kids in a town of a little over 1000, one AED, let alone five, is sometimes unheard of.

I remember doing research about Long QT syndrome. I was thankful for the information and could not believe that this active 4th grade boy had such a life-altering condition. I was also very thankful that he hadn't collapsed on the football field or the basketball court. I definitely became more aware of cardiac events among children and teens.

There were some scary times along the way. One-time Devon went on a student council trip to Kauffman Stadium in Kansas City. I was not aware he was going or that the bus was leaving before normal school hours. When I found out Devon was on a trip without an AED, I made the high school principal drive to meet the bus with one. I was very relieved when it was delivered to him. The next year during our before-school-begins meetings, I gave a harsh reminder to all teachers that they had better let me know who, what, and when students would be out of the building for trips.

I also remember feeling bad for Devon that it seemed his athletic career was over before it began. I told him about Fred Gruhn, a Lincoln Alumni who has a side job doing "table work" for the NAIA college basketball tournament, national championship, DI football, and basketball games, etc. I wanted Devon to know there were other sports-related things he could do. And this last week, he graduated from Quincy University after being the punter for the football program for the past 3 years.

Most of all, it's wonderful to see a healthy, happy college graduate after all these years! I am so proud of Devon and his mom. Angela has worked tirelessly to raise money for cardiac awareness and screenings among youth in west-central Missouri and beyond.

Dr. T. — Devon's Children's Mercy Doctor

For Devon: I want to take this opportunity to express how truly amazed I am by everything you and your family have achieved. When I first met you, you were in shock—scared of the unknown and unsure of what the future held. Your eyes were filled with tears, and your parents were nervous about what would lie ahead. But through the challenges, we built a strong bond, founded on mutual trust. Together, we overcame many hurdles concerning your well-being, and while it wasn't always easy, I watched you grow stronger each time.

It has been a great privilege to witness your transformation—not only into a strong, young athlete but also into a mature young man excelling in academics. Your growth has been inspiring.

Even though I'm no longer your doctor, please know that I'm always here for you and your family. I look forward to hearing about all the amazing things you continue to accomplish and seeing the many milestones you'll share along the way.

With all my love and support, Dr. T.

Joannah — Devon's 4th Grade Teacher

Devon was the ideal student. Perfect in class and worked hard on everything he did. At that point in the school year we had the students grouped together during an extra reading time. He was in the group that went to the library to read with Mrs. Lynde(the librarian). His group was coming back to the classroom. Mrs. Cox and I were standing in the hallway, just to direct traffic.

He was walking right behind another student. I remember watching him fall, and thinking, "That's odd. He must have tripped on the person in front of him." I went to him and put my hand on his shoulder to help him up and he didn't immediately move. That is when it hit me, he didn't just trip. I shook his shoulder and he sorta woke up. He sat up in a daze. I was in shock. Nothing had ever prepared me for a student collapsing right in front of me. I remember Mrs. Cox saying, "Oh my gosh, he needs to go to the nurse!" I had Mrs. Cox watch the kids and I walked him to the nurse. I was questioning myself. Did he hit his head, what just happened? It was a very scary moment.

The rest of the year, I was always worrying about him. In the early days, he wasn't allowed to run or do anything physical. I made up games for the kids to play in the gym that were safe (pack man walking style) so he could play safely. When we were outside, he was always the referee. It was very hard on him. I also remember how amazing the rest of the class was. They all stepped up to support him. They made sure to find ways to include him safely. It was a very scary and rewarding year. I will never forget it.

Jeana — Retired Teacher and Sub

Witnessing students in distress and making the right decisions to help them is a teacher's worst nightmare. Teachers delight in students who are kind, caring, have a good sense of humor, and are enthusiastic in all their endeavors. Devon Parrott was one of the students who exhibited all of those qualities.

I had the privilege of being a long term sub for Mrs. Goosen, one of Devon's 4th grade teachers, during her maternity leave. It was terrifying to witness Devon's collapse in the 4th grade hallway. Joannah, (his home room teacher) immediately went to help Devon while others notified the nurse and principal. Devon's classmates were distraught and very concerned about his wellbeing. Thankfully, Devon's first experience with Long QT syndrome was not a fatal one, as many are.

During the testing process many tears and prayers were shared by Lincoln students and staff. Unfortunately, the LQTS diagnosis changed Devon and his family's lives forever. The Lincoln staff and students were all trained to look for any signs of Devon's potential collapse. Even though all school personnel are trained to protect students, it is terrifying to know that your immediate reactions during a crisis could be a matter of life or death to a person with Long QT syndrome.

Unfortunately, Devon still had a few close calls with death during a movie outing and a surgery to replace an ICD. Prayers again were lifted by the student body, staff, and community. Devon is an amazing young man who has been able to excel scholastically and athletically.

His family, Angela, Jason, and Dawson have channeled their worry about Devon into helping others by sponsoring a 5K. All proceeds go to testing young children for Sudden Arrhythmic Death Syndrome and LQTS. Devon's Beat has helped give other families information through testing that could save their child's life. Did Devon's collapse just change his life? No, It changed everyone associated with Devon.

All of us had a reckoning about the fragility of life and realized that you can continue to have a wonderful life even after a devastating medical diagnosis. Devon taught us that lesson.

Jessica — Family Friend

Angela and I met years ago while running our local communities' youth football leagues. As all small towns go, most of your neighboring teams are rivals. There's always one that's just a little stronger. Windsor and Lincoln were exactly that. Angela's youngest son Dawson and my son Reece are the same age, so they have played football against each other since the age of six. We aren't exactly sure how the rivalry became very strong; maybe it was "that fast Parrott kid" or the fact that their fathers were both of their head coaches. Either way, this sometimes (not so) fun rivalry continued for years.

During this time is when I began to learn more about Devon, the Devon's Beat foundation, and all that Angela was doing to spread awareness to other families. In April of 2020 when Devon had to go back into the hospital is when I and our football family really saw the importance of these screenings for our own kids.

Watching mother to mother was heartbreaking; seeing this family and their community fear the worst as Devon went in for surgery. That is when I committed to bringing Devon's Beat to Windsor.

We hit the ground running. We quickly got multiple donations as we reached out to individuals and businesses to sponsor heart screenings for our own, and those in the future. We were overwhelmed by the response, and so grateful for the support. On 8/29/20 along with Athletic Testing Solutions (My HeartCheck) we were able to screen 58 kids. Of those 58 screenings there were FIVE heart conditions found. Two potentially life threatening; Long QT syndrome and Wolff-Parkinson-White syndrome, two that required follow ups with a Cardiologist, and one that needed to be known for future reference. This was an unbelievable amount of very serious conditions for our small town.

The child diagnosed with WPW Syndrome is our son's best friend. Unfortunately until things hit "close to home" we don't always recognize the importance of something. He was active in year-round sports, a very energetic and "healthy" 12 year old boy, with absolutely NO symptoms! Our community was in shock, to say the least. Luckily and thankfully, because of Devon's Beat, this young man had surgery to repair this defect, and was back on the field playing football before the season ended.

After our results, Angela pitched a two day "Rivals on the Field" screening event to encourage even more neighboring towns to have their kids screened. We were able to secure numerous donations as Windsor's findings spread to parents, families, and businesses alike. On October 17th and 18th, the two day event resulted in screening 109 children. The most to date for Devon's Beat. This event resulted in four findings that required follow ups with a cardiologist. Again, shocking results; but grateful the families now have this knowledge and a plan of action for the future. Not everyone is this lucky. 4,000 young people die each year from the condition Devon has, most with no signs or symptoms at all besides death. Through knowledge, awareness, and understanding the importance of proper testing, this can be preventable. Everyone always thinks, "That's not going to happen to me or my child," until it does. I am forever grateful and thankful for the rivalry that has created the friendship I have with Angela.

Our bond grew much stronger that day through tears and (literal) heartbreak as our entire community waited for one of our very own to get out of surgery. I am very proud of her efforts to write this book and the advocate she is to save lives every day. We may not talk much, or even at all on our boys' game days, but our mama hearts will forever be connected because of Devon's Beat.

Tommy and Presley — Parents of Chase

I had not heard much about Devon's Beat before my friend Jessica brought this amazing group of people to Windsor High School. We were told it was a heart screening.

We just thought, "Ok, why not." At the time, our boys were around 13 and 14 years old respectively. We wanted to help out with the cause and of course make sure our boys were healthy. The boys never had any health issues we were concerned about, or any issues they had complained about. We had absolutely no concerns and never would have thought either boy had any issues at all.

When we left the screening, I do remember Chase, my youngest, asking Parker, my oldest, if his machine was beeping the whole time. Parker said, "No?" Chase said, "Man, my machine was going crazy." I didn't even think anything of it at the time. I guess that should have been my first sign something was wrong. It was maybe 3 days later when I received a call saying that Chase's screening detected Wolff-Parkinson-White-Syndrome (WPW).

I was in shock to say the least. I was told this is potentially a life-threatening heart condition if left untreated. Chase is our athlete of all sports. He is always on the go, so much energy and spunk. He never complained of any symptoms during any of his young athletic career. When they were talking about the next steps, selfishly all I could think about was him not being able to do what he loves… SPORTS!! Luckily, they explained that WPW is a curable condition that can be treated. I have googled the treatment he received to cure his condition.

The primary treatment for Wolff-Parkinson-White (WPW) syndrome is a procedure called catheter ablation. This involves inserting a catheter into a vein and using radiofrequency energy to destroy the extra electrical pathway in the heart causing the abnormal rhythm. The procedure effectively cures most patients with WPW syndrome. This condition is considered a silent killer. Absolutely frightening to hear! You hear of kids that just collapse while playing basketball, football, etc. This is what we could have experienced with our own child. We would have never even known he had the issue until it was too late.

We scheduled an appointment to see a doctor immediately. Before we knew it, he was scheduled for his heart procedure. Everything went smoothly and they were able to cure him of this condition. His recovery time was very minimal. He even was able to join his football team for the last few games of the season.

We will always be forever grateful to Jessica Heany and Angela Parrott for bringing Devon's Beat to Windsor. We will also never forget how much Devon's Beat changed our child's life without even knowing it at the time.

This is such an easy thing to do for your child. They do a wonderful job to keep the screenings affordable and they make the process quick and painless. It was one of the best decisions we have made, as their parents.

I know Devon's Beat is becoming more of a household name now. People are understanding what it is and how it can change lives. Thank you, Angela Parrott, for making this possible for all our local families. You are saving lives, and it is a blessing!!

Chase's Story — Told by his father

We've all been hearing a lot about Devon's Beat, but do you realize how close to home this is to us? Tommy Hampton shared his son's story in an email to chamber members in the hopes of another child's life being saved. He and Presley have allowed me to share that email here, as well. We are all very thankful that Chase's condition was diagnosed when it was.

Chase's Story: My son Chase is just like everyone else's child. The kid is full of energy and hard to tie down. If Devon's Beat had never come to this town we would never have had this screening done. We thought it was a good cause and figured why not have our kids tested. We never expected anything to come back with a positive screening on our child.

When they are bouncing off the walls and showing no signs or symptoms of anything why would you be concerned about anything? Chase plays all sports (Football, baseball, basketball) not to mention all the other activities he does riding bikes and running around. With the condition Devon's Beat screenings found (Wolff-Parkinson-White syndrome) he could have dropped dead at any time. I know that sounds harsh, but that is the reality.

These are the things everyone hears about on the news. Kids all of a sudden drop on the field while playing sports or practicing. No one had a clue anything was wrong with them. That's what this foundation is all about. SAVING KIDS LIVES!

The syndromes they are finding, the kids have no signs or symptoms of. Silent Killers! I thank God that we did this screening and I am very thankful to Angela Parrott, Jessica Heany, and the Devon's Beat foundation for bringing screenings to our town. Although Chase can be a pain sometimes, we could not imagine a world without our son.

Thank you for listening to our story. If anyone wants to talk about it, Presley and I are more than willing to share. Please! If you are able to donate to this great cause, do it!. It doesn't have to just be businesses that donate, individuals can also. We have donated, as well as several of our friends and family members. After seeing how this saved my kids life, and knowing how this can help other families going forward, how could you not support them.

Just so everyone is aware, thankfully, Chase's condition was curable. We had his Procedure at Children's Mercy and he is 100% healthy now! He was released back to start playing football. If that isn't a miracle I do not know what is.

Kerry — Family Friend

We met the Parrott Family in the summer of 2020. Our oldest son Beau was on the same summer ball team as Dawson. As we got to know the Parrott's, we learned the story about Devon. We had met Devon a few times when he came to watch his brother play. It wasn't until Angela organized My HeartCheck and Devon's Beat to come to Springfield and do heart screenings that we really realized the magnitude of Devon's diagnosis.

As we learned more and got to know the Parrott family better, we decided that we wanted to help them as much as possible. We've been donating to Devon's Beat now for 4 years. Devon is an inspiration to so many. He took this potentially life threatening diagnosis and has handled it better than most. All the surgeries and hospital visits and sitting out of athletics is devastating for anyone, but especially an active boy. He has gone on to thrive in football and academics at Quincy University and continued to inspire our family with all his achievements.

Angela and I have grown very close since we've met. Devon is just like her in many ways. She is just as inspiring as her son. Caring, kind, and always putting others first. Her determination and dedication to Devon's Beat and to help as many other kids as she can is to be commended. I am thankful God had our path's cross. I am thankful for her friendship, that I cherish deeply, but also to be a part of something special (even if we are a small part). Devon's Beat and the Parrott family are literally saving kids' lives, one scan at a time. Devon's Beat has been to two schools now that mean a lot to me - Rogersvllle and Monett and I am looking forward to more years to come.

David — My HeartCheck

I first met Devon in 2017 when he was 15. Just 5 years after his diagnosis of Long QT syndrome. He was kind of shy and quiet. His mom,

Angela, always made sure he attended the heart screenings. He never complained—even though it wasn't exactly the most exciting activity for a teenager. I was always impressed by how involved he was willing to be. Even at that young age, it was clear he understood the importance of what we were doing.

One of my favorite memories is convincing Devon to do short, live videos on social media to help spread awareness about heart screenings. At first, we'd do them together, and I could tell it wasn't his favorite thing. With a little encouragement, he began taking control and doing them on his own—and he did such a great job! Watching him grow into that confidence was incredibly rewarding.

Angela's commitment to Devon's Beat has been nothing short of extraordinary. This really struck me during a HeartCheck event in December 2024, organized in partnership with Devon's Beat. Remarkably, it took place on the same day Devon graduated from college. It was a day of incredible milestones—celebrating Devon's achievement while providing life-saving tests for other families.

I hope Angela and Devon know how much of an impact they've had—not just on My HeartCheck, but on me personally. Their dedication has been a constant source of motivation and a powerful reminder of why we do what we do. To date, Devon's Beat and My HeartCheck have provided free youth heart screenings to nearly 2,000 kids. That's nearly 2,000 lives potentially changed, thanks to this amazing partnership—and we're not done yet! I'm very grateful to be part of this journey with them.

Eric — from My HeartCheck

I first learned about Devon through a Facebook post made by his mother in 2016. She shared something on the LQTS Kids & Families page. While I can't recall the exact content, I felt compelled to reach out. Initially, I didn't get a response. When I did, it led My HeartCheck to embark on a journey resulting in over 30 heart screening events since 2017.

In my first encounter with Devon, he was somewhat shy, but willing to talk about his condition. Most kids would be angry or shut down with a hand like he was dealt. I was very impressed with how grown-up he seemed about it. He was taking it in stride, which I would later learn was his style. It didn't take long for us to form a friendship. He always called me "old man," which allowed me to respond with a witty remark of my own (I have plenty of those).

For the first few years, Devon attended most of the screenings and talked to kids coming in for the heart screening. Eventually, we even got him to do Facebook Live posts to discuss the importance of the screening that was taking place.

Devon is a person who combines kindness and confidence. I believe he will succeed in whatever he chooses to pursue. I will always cherish the pleasure of having met Devon.

LeeAnn — Family Friend

Angela and I became fast friends as soon as the Parrott's moved to Lincoln in 2003. I had just opened my insurance office and Angela was selling Avon. She would come into the office to sell her Skin so Soft and we would ultimately end up talking for hours. Devon was just a year old and usually in tow.

Our office visits turned to daily lunch outings and shopping trips. While Devon was just a couple months younger than my son, Jackson, Devon was in the grade below. Devon was on our youth football team every other year as the age groups were 1/2, 3/4, and 5/6 grade. We also pulled him up to play basketball on our team until he was old enough and they started a team of their age group.

Because of how close we were, it was nothing unusual that I asked her to go shopping one December day in 2012. I remember her calling to tell me the school had called and he had passed out. I reassured her with any reason I could think of, as to why that could have happened. She immediately took him to the pediatrician and, out of an abundance of caution, he wanted to have him checked at Children's Mercy.

The day we went shopping I remember Angela purchasing all the normal gifts for a 10 year old boy, particularly a basketball and video games. While we were shopping, she got the call that they had an appointment for the following day. All the while, still not thinking this could possibly be anything more than dehydration, no one could have prepared for the news they received at the visit.

At the time, little was known about Long QT syndrome. The biggest take away was that Devon couldn't play sports. That was devastating to everyone involved. Sports were such a huge part of their lives. Angela also thought she had to return the gifts she bought. At the time, they didn't think he could even play video games due to the stimulation. It seemed that life as Devon knew it was over.

As the initial shock wore off and we were all doing research on this condition we'd never heard of before, we were learning about SADS and athletic heart screenings. I made some calls to St Luke's heart institute to inquire about the process of getting screenings. I didn't really get very far with that call, but we were determined to make something happen. I told Angela "You're going to turn this into something positive." That she did, immediately getting to work and finding someone that would do heart screenings.

That first screening she had in Clinton, both of my kids were the first to sign up. Since then my son has had three! It was scary and some parents didn't want to do it. They were afraid of what the results would be. I have to admit, I was afraid too and the prospect of my kids not playing sports and changing our lives was frightening.

Devon's Beat was formed as a fundraiser to bring another screening to our school and give those who couldn't pay the ability to have the screenings for free. Devon's Beat exploded and the community rallied for this great cause. Twelve years later and it's still going strong.

As time went on those screenings expanded to area schools and even branched out to schools in Southwest Missouri and Arkansas. With the money raised through Devon's Beat, all screenings have been free. I'm sure Angela has a count of the number of screenings done but it is the hundreds or thousands. Several lives have been saved from those screenings.

Through the years, Devon's life has definitely changed. Luckily the first information coming from the Doctor after the diagnosis was altered and Devon did get to resume sports. He has gone on to get to experience high school and college the same as any other 22 year old. Even going above and beyond that, and playing College Football! It truly is a story of making lemonade from lemons and along the way touching the lives of so many others.

Krista — Family Friend

When I first met the Parrotts, I had no idea the impact this special family would have on my life. Rewind to the summer of 2018. My oldest son, Drew, attended kicking lessons with Devon at SKP with Coach David Brader. One afternoon, my husband, Andy, came home after practice and mentioned that Devon was going to stay with us for a week over the summer so he could attend extra lessons. Since the Parrotts lived in Lincoln, MO, and our house was closer, it made sense.

I gladly agreed, but then Andy casually added, "Oh, I forgot to tell you! Devon has a heart condition, but he has an internal AED, so it'll be no big deal!" I immediately asked for more details, and Andy must have sensed the panic in my voice. A heart condition? What if something happened while he was here? How would I even know what to do? He reassured me, explaining what a great family the Parrott's were, and added, "Nothing has happened to his heart for a LONG time!" Still, I needed more information.

I agreed to talk to Angela, Devon's mom, and decide from there whether or not I was comfortable with the situation. Fast forward to a week later. Angela called, and within less than 60 seconds, I knew Devon would be staying with us. We immediately clicked, sharing the same hopes and dreams for our boys as well as the same worries and concerns. Our conversation lasted about an hour, but it felt like I had known her for years.

When Devon came to stay, he fit right in. My initial worries about his heart condition faded, and he quickly felt like one of my own boys. I had a plan in my head in case anything happened, but instead, I simply enjoyed having him with us and doing all the fun things our family loves.

Angela took the time to educate me about Devon's condition and encouraged me to have Drew and my younger son, Carter, screened at one of her events. Drew was immediately cleared, but Carter's results were inconclusive. Angela could sense my fear and quickly asked the screeners to take a second look. Later, I received a call confirming that Carter's heart was healthy. Her compassion and support during that moment meant the world to me.

Our families stayed in touch, attending Devon's Beat 5Ks, celebrations, and even his state football game. Any chance we got, we spent time together and continued to talk regularly.

I vividly remember the day we realized our boys would fulfill their dream of playing collegiate football at Quincy University—and they would be roommates! My mama heart couldn't have been happier, and I knew our bond with Angela, Jason, Devon and Daws would only grow stronger.

We celebrated the great times and supported one another through the tough ones. Drew and Devon have now graduated from QU and begun their journeys into adulthood. Devon remains a bright and courageous young man whose energy and smile light up every room, no matter the challenges he has faced. Angela and Jason have always exuded warmth and kindness, making it easy to feel at home in their presence.

The love and connection we share reminds me that family isn't just about blood relatives; it's about the people who choose to walk beside you, no matter what. I will forever be grateful that Devon decided to spend that week at our home. It was the start of a lifelong friendship and a bond that feels just like family.

Ellen — Jace's Mom
(Basketball player from Marshall, Missouri)

It was in a dark hospital room that I received a message from Angela. At that time I felt like I was on an island. With all the information, the doctors, the beeps of the machines and an almost adult son with no idea what he was facing. Quickly the warm words that no mother ever wants to hear but also very thankful to hear. "My son also had an issue. I'm here for you!" It was February 9, 2023.

To date I have a huge amount of love and respect for Angela but still haven't been able to meet face to face. I have contacted her to collaborate in our community to help reach and save others. Without hesitation her answer is always "Let's do it!" You know I never knew I needed moms like Angela. But God continually puts her in my path when I need her, even to write about this. It was the perfect timing. She offers this great service for children to have early screening but she also is a sounding board for so many mommas that need to breathe while facing the challenges that come with this diagnosis. I am blessed to love Angela and everything she stands for!

Kim — Kane's mom

On Wednesday, June 19, we received the call that would change our lives forever. Our 15-year-old son, Kane, took part in a free heart screening through My HeartCheck, thanks to the generosity of the Parrott and Lance families. Although we had no prior concerns about Kane's heart, we felt led by God to have him tested, especially with the rise of cardiac arrests among young athletes. The results revealed concerns, and we were advised to immediately take Kane to a cardiologist and to stop all sports until cleared.

The following day, with Eric's help at My HeartCheck, we were able to get Kane into a cardiologist. After further tests, including genetic screening, we were informed that Kane might never be able to play basketball again. Just over a week later, Kane was diagnosed with genetic Long QT syndrome, Type 3. While the news was heavy, we knew we were blessed to catch it early—many families don't have that opportunity. We believed God placed the right people in our path to save Kane's life.

Just two months after the diagnosis, God worked miracles, and the beta blockers were effective. Kane's QT intervals were within the normal range, and he was cleared to resume all sports and activities. Kane's favorite scripture, John 13:7, perfectly reflects his trust in God's plan during this challenging time. Though we didn't fully understand what was happening, we knew God's purpose would be revealed in His timing. Kane's journey deepened his faith and gave us all a greater understanding of God's miraculous timing.

We continue to be inspired by Kane's unwavering faith. Angela and Devon's story not only helped save our son's life but also led us through one of the most challenging seasons our family has ever faced. Their ongoing support brings us comfort and hope, reminding us that we don't have to face this diagnosis alone. I believe God will use Kane's story to impact many lives, just as Devon's has. We are grateful to God for the Parrott family and their courage in continuing to share their story.

ABOUT THE AUTHORS

ANGELA PARROTT is a mom to Devon and Dawson and a wife to Jason, first and foremost. She is also the founder and operator of Devon's Beat foundation. Devon's Beat was established in 2013 after Devon was diagnosed with Long QT syndrome. The sole purpose for Angela was to establish Devon's Beat to raise awareness and funds for families to screen their kids for any sudden arrhythmic death syndromes. Angela's work continues to this day.

TYRAN PAYNE is a lifelong educator of over 30 years. He was one of Devon's teachers in junior high school in Lincoln, Missouri. Tyran is also a published author and certified publishing consultant. His goal is to help write and publish books, like this one, that are geared toward helping the greater good in humanity. Tyran and his wife Amanda have dedicated their lives to education.

www.ingramcontent.com/pod-product-compliance
Lightning Source LLC
Chambersburg PA
CBHW021136130626
46554CB00005B/1536